the archaeology of hamilton county ohio

by s.f. starr

Copyright © 1960 by S. Frederick Starr. Copyright © 2019 by S. Frederick Starr. Published by Commonwealth Book Company. All Rights Reserved. Printed in the United States of America.

ISBN: 9781948986083

Commonwealth
BOOK COMPANY
St. Martin, Ohio

The University of Michigan Memorial — Phoenix Project Radiocarbon Laboratory under the direction of H. R. Crane has determined the dates for the following samples:

M-910 Haffner-Kuntz Site, Little Miami River, Ohio   1375 ± 150 yr.

    Charcoal from bottom of layer of shell and bone 4 ft. below surface, associated with Fort Ancient pottery.   *S. Frederick Starr.*

M-907 Turpin Farm Site, Hamilton Co., Ohio   675 ± 150 yr.

    Log 36 in. below surface of refuse pit, associated with Fort Ancient pottery.   *James Chapman.*

This information was received from the Museum of Anthropology at the University of Michigan in Ann Arbor, Michigan.

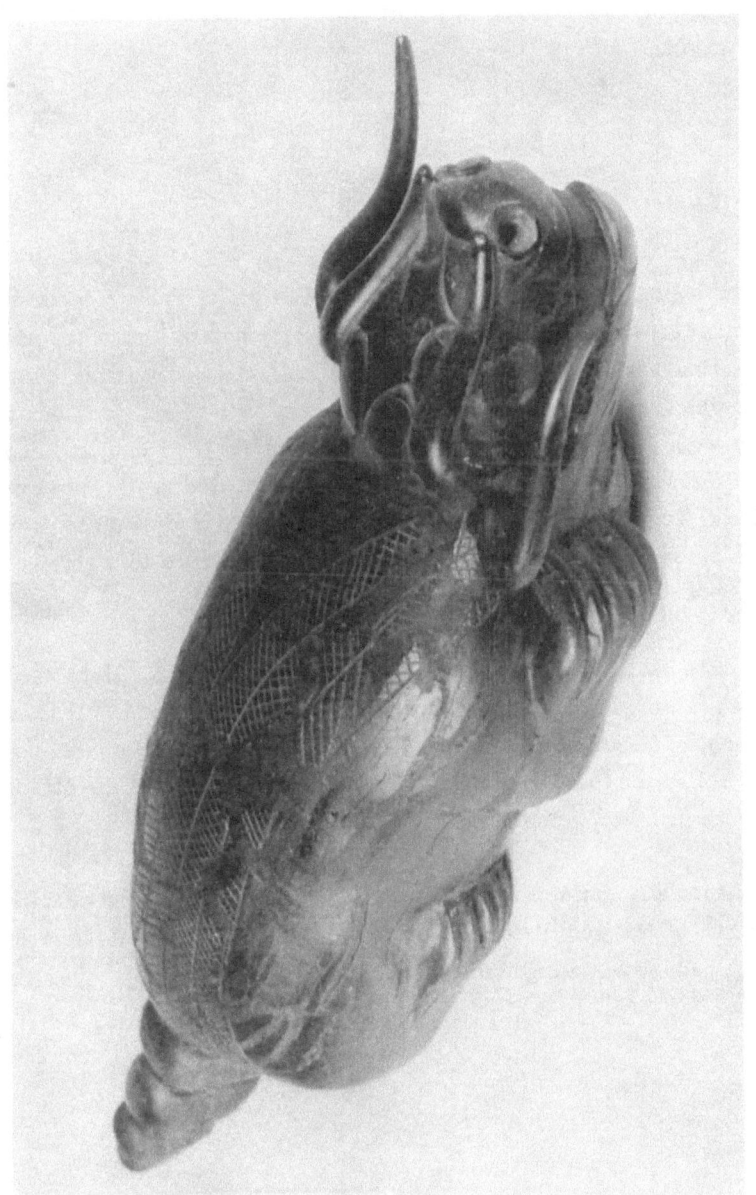

'Monster' Effigy from the Turner Works, Anderson Township
(Peabody Museum, Cambridge)

ACKNOWLEDGMENTS

Archaeological survey work directly involves all of the residents of the particular area being surveyed. The surveyor's most valuable sources of information are the seriously interested collectors and those older residents who know the countryside in which they live. Hamilton County has many such residents to whom we are grateful for their courtesy and interest. Messrs. Charles B. Winter of North Bend, George Hayhurst of Sayler Park, Tony Collins of Fernald, George Hack of Madisonville, and Gene Schlosser of Cincinnati all gave much of their time to walk over large areas of the county with us.

Dr. James H. Kellar, Dr. James B. Griffin, Dr. Glenn A. Black, and Mr. Ellis Crawford very kindly gave valuable advice. Dr. Stephen Williams of the Peabody Museum in Cambridge was of great help in analyzing the priceless collection there. Mr. Eric G. Carlson capably handled the photographic work involved in the survey, and aided in the compilation of data.

I am especially grateful to Mr. Ralph E. Dury, director of the Cincinnati Museum of Natural History. His constant and personal interest in the survey made it an unforgettable educational experience.

TABLE OF CONTENTS

I. Background and Scope of the Survey

   Geography and Topography

II. The Paleo-Indian Occupation of the Southwestern Ohio Area

   Adena Circular Earthworks

   Ceremonial Earthworks

   Defensive Fortifications

   Stone Mounds

III. Additional Mounds and Village Sites in Anderson Township

   Additional Mounds and Village Sites in Columbia Township

   Additional Mounds and Village Sites in Symmes Township

   Additional Mounds and Village Sites in Sycamore Township

   Additional Mounds and Village Sites in Springfield Township

   Additional Mounds and Village Sites in Cincinnati

   Additional Mounds and Village Sites in Delhi Township

   Additional Mounds and Village Sites in Miami Township

   Additional Mounds and Village Sites in Green and Colerain Townships

   Additional Mounds and Village Sites in Crosby Township

   Additional Mounds and Village Sites in Harrison Township

   Additional Mounds and Village Sites in Whitewater Township

IV. Bibliography of Works on Hamilton County Prehistory and Collections of Artifacts.

BACKGROUND AND SCOPE OF THE SURVEY

The physical remains of prehistoric populations in Hamilton County have long attracted curiosity. In the past one hundred and fifty years, hundreds of people have accidently or intentionally dug into mounds and village sites and have been well rewarded for their efforts. Fortunately, the ancient remains have aroused enough attention so that many individuals and organizations have attempted to catalogue surviving sites before they were destroyed. Other groups have undertaken the excavation of mounds and earthworks. Although most of the early work suffered from inaccuracy and, particularly in the nineteenth century, from a lack of adequate background knowledge, reports of past surveys and excavations are valuable, for they often yield the sole account of destroyed sites.

Dr. Daniel Drake, widely known as the founder of the Cincinnati Medical College, was one of the first observers to note the archaeological wealth of the area. His *Picture of Cincinnati* contains accurate accounts of many earthworks, located in what is now the downtown area. Whether or not Dr. Drake might have gone further afield if he had had the transportation facilities cannot be ascertained and is not important; we are, in any case, indebted to him for his work in the Basin area.

Like Dr. Drake, President William Henry Harrison confined his archaeological interest to the neighborhood in which he lived. As a military man, his interest centered around Miami Fort which crowns the hilltop behind his old home. Harrison's speculations as to the "Azteck" origin of the moundbuilders are ill-informed, but his measurements of the fort were competent indeed and his interest was genuine.

Squire and Davis were the first outsiders to take an active interest in Hamilton County's rich prehistory. Their *Ancient Monuments of the Mississippi Valley*, published in 1848, contains numerous references to local sites, many of which are now destroyed. They were concerned only with the larger mounds and earthworks, but their report, issued by the Smithsonian Institution, is admirably comprehensive in view of the great area covered by the authors many years before modern roads and the automobile.

The most recent survey of the entire county was made by William C. Mills in 1914. It suffers greatly from inaccuracy. Mills is said to have based his survey on postcard replies to questionnaires sent to mailmen throughout the state. The shortcomings of such a method are obvious. While Mills' map gives some idea of the concentration of sites, it is useless for scientific purposes because of the grotesque exaggeration in the scale of the symbols; a single mound, for instance, will appear to extend for half a mile.

The most accurate of the early surveyors was Dr. Charles L. Metz of Madisonville, Cincinnati. His survey of Anderson Township and parts of Columbia Township, conducted in the 1870's and early 1880's, contains practically every mound and village site accessible at the time. Metz was the Commanding General of an army of amateurs who resided in the Madisonville area. Messrs. Hill, Low, Cox and Langdon spent their weekends exploring local archaeological sites. In Metz's correspondence frequent reference is made to expeditions begun as early as three o'clock in the morning. The records of the Literary and Scientific Society of Madisonville perpetuate the well-directed efforts of these men. Many of their carefully prepared reports, published in the Journal of the Society, testify to the high calibre of their work and show that they were not mere weekend dilettantes. Unfortunately, their interest was primarily in the artifacts. More than one account describes the group standing about a burial site at Madisonville, eagerly waiting to snatch its contents for their parlor cabinets. Although their work lacked the complete precision and thoroughness of modern excavations, they recovered thousands of valuable artifacts which might otherwise have been lost. These discoveries aroused the interest of the Peabody Museum of Harvard University in the little Miami region, which resulted in many well-documented excavations, many of which were conducted by Dr. Metz; but by the 1920's, Harvard began to look elsewhere for archaeological sites.

The Cincinnati Museum of Natural History has been excavating locally since the nineteenth century. In the last twelve years it has adopted a new archaeological program and has excavated much on the Turpin Site and the Sayler Park Mound.

The destruction of archaeological sites is continuing at such a rapid pace that the classical archaeological approach of "attack the best sites first" has become impractical and must give way to a program of salvage archaeology. In keeping with these needs, the Board of Commissioners of Hamilton County and the Cincinnati Museum of Natural History have co-sponsored this survey to locate sites which may be explored before they are obliterated.

The present survey was made in the summer of 1958, with the exception of Anderson Township which was surveyed in the years 1956-57. Representative areas within each geographic section of the county (i.e., hilltops above the Ohio or the east side of the Great Miami valley between Dunlap and Harrison Pike) and those areas which showed the greatest potential were thoroughly examined, while only the more promising areas were checked in the remainder of the county. Those regions of the City of Cincinnati which are densely covered by homes and industry were ignored, with the exception of previously known sites. Naturally, many areas in which certain sites might be located could not be checked, while other sites could not be recognized due to dense ground covering and heavy foliage.

Each site located was measured, mapped and photographed. Records were made of its state of preservation, the owner's address and his attitude toward excavation. In addition, each owner was asked to notify the Museum should his site be threatened with destruction.

The "33" which prefixes each site number refers to Ohio. "Ha." in the trinomial refers to Hamilton County, while the final number designates the specific component in the order in which it was recorded. All sites from 33-Ha.-146 to 33-Ha.-235 have been destroyed, as have a few which follow 33-Ha.-235.

The important sites are listed by two methods. Those sites whose similarity of appearance lends itself readily to comparison are discussed as a group. In the case of many Woodland villages discovered, we do not feel qualified to attempt to classify the sites by relative chronological position within the Woodland period. The cultural associations of most unexcavated mounds are unascertainable except in the few instances where artifacts from these mounds indicative of the builders have previously been found. Therefore, following Section I are brief descriptions of the previously unrecorded mounds and villages in each township. The reader may, from the data presented, draw his own conclusions as to the cultural affinities of the individual sites.

147 earth mounds	48 existing; 99 excavated or destroyed
20 stone mounds	6 existing; 14 excavated or destroyed
14 Adena circular earthworks	3 existing; 10 excavated or destroyed
3 fortifications	3 existing
8 ceremonial earthworks	2 existing; 6 excavated or destroyed
11 cemeteries	3 existing; 8 excavated or destroyed
4 borrow pits	4 destroyed
88 villages or campsites	81 existing; 7 excavated or destroyed
295 prehistoric sites	146 existing; 148 excavated or destroyed

GEOGRAPHY AND TOPOGRAPHY

Hamilton County is located at the southwestern corner of Ohio. It is bordered by Indiana on the west, on the south by Kentucky, Clermont County lies to the east and Warren and Butler Counties are to the north.

The geographical situation of Hamilton County is admirably suited to the needs of a modern community. The valleys formed by the Ohio, Great and Little Miami, Whitewater and Mill Creek, and the hills which surround them were equally attractive to the prehistoric men who inhabited the region in great numbers. Since game and food abounded in the area, geographical preference was the chief criterion in considering locations for a village site. The valleys were apparently preferred to hilly land in most areas of the county.

On the southern boundary of the county, the Ohio River runs in a trough confined by the high hills which come down nearly to its banks. Only in the extreme eastern area, the Cincinnati Basin, and at Sayler Park are there level plains or terraces broad enough for comfortable habitation.

For the greater part of its course through the county, the Great Miami is also confined by hills, but for short sections, such as that at Dunlap, its valley broadens. After it joins the Whitewater River, which flows in a broad valley from Dearborn County, Indiana, the Miami meanders through a level plain. Level, elevated terraces on both sides of the river were often chosen for village sites.

The Little Miami follows much the same pattern. Beginning at the eastern boundary of the County, it flows through a narrow valley until it meets the East Fork near Terrace Park. From the point of junction until it reaches the Ohio, the Little Miami follows a wandering course which has changed greatly in the past hundred and fifty years and is a constant flood problem to the valley residents. Only the raised terraces are a safe refuge from floods.

The highly industrialized Mill Creek valley runs south to the Ohio at the center of Cincinnati, forming the large plain of Cincinnati. In its northern sections, the Mill Creek valley is flanked by low, rolling hills instead of the steep and relatively high hills which characterize the valleys of the Ohio and the Miamis. The large area between the Great Miami and Mill Creek is very much eroded by dozens of creeks, leaving little of the original nine hundred foot till-plain intact. East from Mill Creek in Sycamore Township the glacial till plain is unbroken by "recent" erosion; few streams criss-cross this area. Neither the mature typography of the Colerain-Green-Delhi Township region nor the high level land of Sycamore Township were well fitted to the Indians' needs. Upland Anderson Township, however, has both the steep gradients common in the western side of the county, and the level till-plains which characterize Sycamore Township. The union of these two features has produced a topography which answered all of the geographical needs of a primitive society.

Hamilton County has within its borders high hills, which provided game and protection from enemies, and level "bottoms" on which sedentary agricultural communities could thrive. The utilization of topographical and geographical features gives important clues to a society's needs. The reader should be mindful of this fact as he studies the prehistory of Hamilton County.

THE PALEO-INDIAN OCCUPATION OF THE SOUTH-WESTERN OHIO AREA

The earliest evidences of man in Hamilton County are the so-called Folsom points. These distinctive projectile points have been found everywhere in the United States east of the Rockies and have been proved to be of great antiquity, some reaching as far back as 12,000 years and more. The location of nearly all fluted points found east of the Mississippi suggests that the points were lost while hunting rather than left at campsites. However, a very few "Folsom" campsites such as the Schoop site in Pennsylvania and the Reagen component in Vermont do exist in the East.

Hamilton County has produced six known "Folsom" field finds and one possible campsite. The present survey has located thirteen other fluted points; four from Dearborn County, Indiana, four from Butler County, Ohio, four from Boone County, Kentucky, and one from Campbell County, Kentucky.

Of the six local finds, the first is in the Charles B. Winter Collection, and is known to be from Miami Township, but is otherwise uncatalogued. The projectile is nearly parallel-sided with a length of 3-5/8" and a width of 1-1/8". The material is a dark, grainy chert. Channel flakes extend one inch up both faces, but grinding is evident only on the concave base. The sides flare outward very slightly at the base, to form noticeably projecting ears.

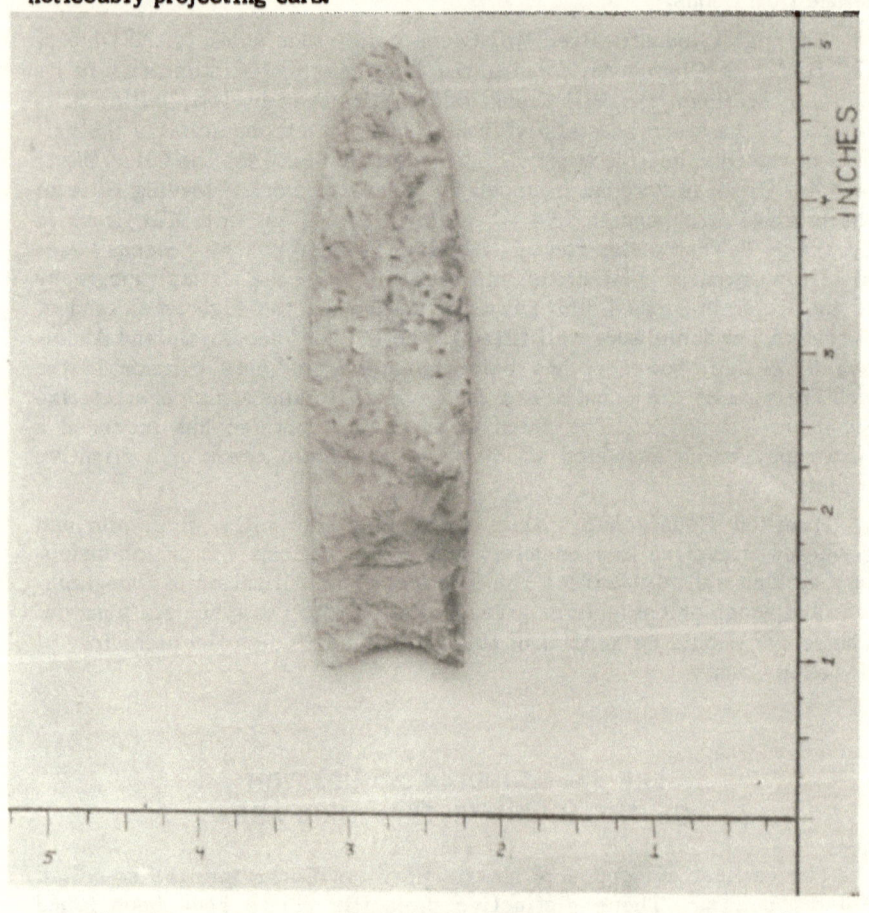

Fluted Point from the Ebersole Site 33-Ha-3, Anderson Township
(Behrman Collection)

The second was found over thirty years ago by Mr. A. Behrman in the immediate area of 33-Ha.-3 in Anderson Township. Whether or not it was found on the site itself cannot be determined, but it is known definitely to be from the low bottom lands at the confluence of the Ohio and Little Miami River. Its length is 4-1/16", width 1-1/8" at the widest point; fluting extends 1-3/8" on one side and only 3/4" on the other. Two channel flakes were removed in preparation for the final deep flute. The straight, tapering sides are ground for 1-3/4", while the concave base is entirely ground. The material is a shiny unweathered chert.

Two fluted points in the Schlosser Collection are from the Little Miami region of Hamilton County, but are otherwise undocumented. The material of which one is made is a peculiar mottled grey shiny chert, speckled with red; it is unlike any local material. It is nearly parallel sided, with shallow flutes extending one-third of the length of the short point. A gradual tapering from base to point characterizes the other.

Another Folsomoid point came from the Madisonville area. Its shape is similar to the untapered point from the Little Miami Valley in the Schlosser Collection.

The last isolated fluted point from Hamilton County was found west of the Atomic Energy Plant and north of Fernald in Crosby Township. A lancelate point from this area will be discussed later. The material from which the fluted point is made is very similar to Flint Ridge flint and the point is concave on both sides.

At 33-Ha.-71 in Anderson Township, Woodland pottery and projectile points are found in the foot-thick overburden while Paleo-Indian artifacts have occasionally been found in the yellow clay below the Woodland level. The topography conforms to the pattern defined by Richey[1] and Witthoft[2] — elevated situations which often command extensive views. From the level hilltop stretches the finest view of the Little Miami Valley obtainable in Hamilton County. Springs abound in the area, but the grassy hilltop is fast eroding along the well-worn bridle paths. In these eroded gullies, the surveyors found most of the artifacts and flakes which are described below.

The artifact collection from the yellow clay level consists of four flakes, one scraper, and three points. The material from which all the pieces are flaked is a creamy to blue-gray chert which exhibits varying degrees of weathering. Unlike the other Hamilton County points, the three from this site are quite short and of a more truly Folsomoid character; one has pronounced ears and slight fluting, the second has pronounced ears also, but is narrower in outline, while the last is more nearly parallel-sided and is fluted for nearly its whole length on both faces. The most deeply fluted of the three was discovered in the collection left by a farmer who had found it nearly a century ago on 33-Ha.-71, protruding from the yellow clay in a gully left by a summer washout. Another point was collected from "three feet below the surface" by a friend of Dr. Metz. This specimen, only recently brought to light in the Peabody Museum's collection, is typically short, but in other respects quite unlike the other two. The material of which it is made is much darker and less weathered than the others and the sides are slightly outward-sloping to the base in contrast to the tapered design of the others. The scraper is 1-1/16" long, rather thick, and quite crudely worked. There can be no doubt that it is made of the same material as the points and that it was

---

[1] Ritchie, William A., *Traces of Early Man in the Northeast.* New York State Museum and Science Service, Bulletin Number 358, June, 1957; p. 7.

[2] Witthoft, John, *A Paleo-Indian Site in Eastern Pennsylvania, An Early Huntint Culture.* Proceedings of the American Philosophical Society, Volume 96, Number 4, August, 1952; p. 485.

found at the same depth. Due to the dense ground covering on this site, only an excavation will prove whether it is a true Folsom campsite.

Fluted Point from 33-Ha-71. (Peabody Museum, Cambridge)

Artifacts from 33-Ha-71
1. Lower – fluted points; 2. Center – scraper;
3. Top and center, right and left – flakes.

Four cream-colored chert Folsomoid points from Mason, in Warren County, Ohio, are in the Bryant Collection at the Cincinnati Museum of Natural History. Whether or not they were all found on the same site cannot be determined.

The first is 2-1/16" long, reaching the widest point near the center and tapering to 15/16" at the concave base. It is fluted on one side and ground both on the base and the edges. Two others, 1-5/8" and 1-29/32" long respectively, are very similar. Both are fluted 3/4" on one side only, and are similar in outline to the larger specimen from 33-Ha.-71.

The last point from Mason is probably of much later origin. Although it exhibits basal grinding and a Folsomoid outline, fluting is lacking and a section of the weathered nodule is also visible. We are unacquainted with any other fluted or Folsomoid points on which the outer surfaces of the nodule have not been worked off.

From neighboring Dearborn County in Indiana came four fluted points in the A. Behrman Collection. All were found in unidentified locations along Laughery Creek. One is similar to those from Mason, another appears to be a fluted lancelate point. Long channel flakes, and the absence of basal concavity characterize a third point, which is 4-3/32" long. The fourth point in the Behrman Collection may have been reworked in the later Archaic period. On this hypothesis, the projectile point was originally over 4" long, concave at the base, and slightly flaring outward to pronounced ears. Approximately 3/4" from the base on the sides is a slight tapering which suggests the slightly stemmed type of Archaic point. The fluting is distinct and there is no patination by which a possible reworking can be verified.

Boone County has produced four fluted points. One, from Camp Ernst on Gunpowder Creek, is a fluted lancelate point, while the other three conform more nearly to the typical Folsom type.

The fluted lancelate point is similar in all respects to the one from the Laughery Creek area. It was found near the village of Hamilton in Boone County. The weathered projectile point is fluted for three-quarters of its length of 3-3/4", and is grooved on the base and up 1" on the edges.

The other three are 2-3/4", 2-1/2" and 2-1/2" long, respectively. The other dimensions are proportionate, producing similar outlines. The longest (i.e., the 2-3/4") is ground only on the base, but both of the others have edge and basal grinding. The longest point was found below Camp Ernst on Gunpowder Creek; one of the other two was found on the hills "near Union"; the other is from the same area but to the east of Union.

On the high hill above the steel mill on Route 177 in Campbell County, Kentucky, a fluted point was found which is now in the collection of the Behringer Museum. It is 2-1/2" long, 7/8" wide, and is fluted for three-fourths of its length. Like the Gunpowder Creek point, it is made from a shiny dark gray flint.

Other fluted points have been found in the Tri-State area, but insufficient data and lack of time have prevented us from cataloguing them. In the future, much greater concern should be shown in recording the precise location at which these rare artifacts are found. Only through the most accurate and meticulous work will the earliest pre-history of the area become clear.

ADENA CIRCULAR EARTHWORKS

Within the limits of Hamilton County were located thirteen of the small circular earthworks around a central mound, of the type attributed by Webb and Snow to the Adena People.[1] Their great age (around two-thousand years) and the large number of them in the county would make them a valuable source of knowledge on the early sedentary cultures, but unfortunately, only the central mound of one (33-Ha.-166) is still visible. That work was one of a pair along Drake Road in Indian Hill. Metz, in a manuscript addendum to a copy of his "Ancient Monuments of the Little Miami Valley", wrote:

> "It consisted of a circular embankment about three feet

---

[1] Webb, William Snyder, *The Adena People*. University of Kentucky, Reports in Anthropology and Archaeology, Vol. VI. Lexington, 1945; pp. 29-33.

FOLSOMOID AND FLUTED POINTS FROM THE TRI-STATE AREA

State	County and Township	Locus	Terrain	Material	Length	Base	Widest Point	Fluting	Grinding	No.	Owner
Ohio	Hamilton Anderson	33 – Ha. – 71	high level hilltop – commanding extensive view.	slightly weathered tan chert	2-1/8"	7/8"	1-1/16"	11/16" on one side – 3/4" on other.	1-17/32" both edges, base, and lower faces.	1.	Cincinnati Museum of Natural History
Ohio	Hamilton Anderson	33 – Ha. – 71	high level hilltop – commanding extensive view.	similar to the above point, but not as weathered and slightly grey.	2-7/16"	13/16"	1-1/32"	1-3/8" on one side; 1-1/16" on other.	1" on both edges and base.	2.	Cincinnati Museum of Natural History
Ohio	Hamilton Anderson	33 – Ha. – 71	high level hilltop – commanding extensive view.	dark grey shiny flint with scattered imperfections on its surface.	2-1/4"	3/4"	3/4"	1-1/2" on one side; 1-3/8" on other.	base and both edges approx. 3/4".	3.	Peabody Museum Cambridge Massachusetts
Ohio	Hamilton Miami	somewhere on the upland area.	high range of hills above Ohio or Miami Rivers.	dark grey, grainy chert.	3-5/8"	1-1/8"	1-1/8"	1" on both sides.	base only.	4.	Mr. Charles B. Winter, North Bend, Ohio.
Ohio	Hamilton Columbia	Little Miami Valley	Unknown	shiny, brown flint	2-1/4"	7/8"	7/8"	1" one side; 1-3/8" on other.	base and 1" both edges.	5.	Mr. Gene Schlosser Cincinnati.

FOLSOMOID AND FLUTED POINTS FROM THE TRI-STATE AREA

State	County and Township	Locus	Terrain	Material	Length	Base	Widest Point	Fluting	Grinding	No.	Owner
Ohio	Hamilton	Little Miami Valley	Unknown	mottled, speckled dark grey to tan with red.	2-1/4"	7/8"	1-1/16"	1" one side; 7/8" other side.	base and 1-3/8" one edge; 1-1/4" other edge.	6.	Mr. Gene Schlosser, Cincinnati
Ohio	Hamilton Anderson	on or near 33 – Ha. – 3	Level bottoms near mouth of Little Miami.	light grey mottled hard chert.	4-1/16"	15/16"	1-1/8"	1-3/8" one side; 3/4" on other side.	base and 1-3/4" of both edges.	7.	Cincinnati Museum of Natural History
Ohio	Hamilton Crosby	west of Atomic Energy Plant near Fernald.	Unknown	shiny, thin well-worked bluish to tan	2-1/8"	15/16"	1-1/8"	3/4" one side; 5/8" on other side.	base and 1" one edge; 1-1/16" other edge.	8.	Mr. Gene Schlosser, Cincinnati
Ohio	Hamilton Columbia	around Madisonville (Cincinnati)	rolling hills, upland	grey, very mottled, slightly weathered chert	2-3/8"	1-1/16"	1-1/16"	1-7/16" one side; 1-3/16" other side.	base and 1-1/8" other 1-3/16" other edge.	9.	Mr. Gene Schlosser, Cincinnati
Ohio	Warren Deerfield	in or near Mason	Unknown	light tan, soft worn chert	2-1/16"	15/16"	1-1/16"	very slightly on one side; none on other.	none	10.	Cincinnati Museum of Natural History

FOLSOMOID AND FLUTED POINTS FROM THE TRI-STATE AREA

State	County and Township	Locus	Terrain	Material	Length	Base	Widest Point	Fluting	Grinding	No.	Owner
Ohio	Warren Deerfield	in or near Mason	unknown	light grey mottled chert	1-29/32"	3/4"	15/16"	none on one side 3/4" on other.	none	11.	Cincinnati Museum of Natural History
Ohio	Warren Deerfield	in or near Mason	unknown	light grey mottled chert	1-5/8"	15/16"	1-1/32"	none on one side 3/4" on other.	base and 1-1/8" of both edges.	12.	Cincinnati Museum of Natural History
Ohio	Warren Deerfield	in or near Mason	unknown	light tan chert showing edge of nodule in one place.	2"	1-1/16"	base (1-1/16")	none	base and 1-1/8" both edge.	13.	Cincinnati Museum of Natural History
Indiana	Dearborn	Laughery Creek Valley (approx.)	valley near small creek	unknown	4-1/8"	1-1/16"	1-1/2"	2-1/2" on one side; 1-3/4" on other.	base and 1-3/4" on one edge; 2" on other edge.	14.	Mr. A. Behrman, Cincinnati
Indiana	Dearborn	Laughery Creek Valley (approx.)	valley near small creek	unknown	2"	1"	1"	9/16" on both sides.	none	15.	Mr. A. Behrman, Cincinnati
Indiana	Dearborn	Laughery Creek Valley (approx.)	valley near small creek	unknown	3-1/2"	9/16"	1"	5/16" on both sides.	base, 1-13/16" both edges.	16.	Mr. A. Behrman, Cincinnati

FOLSOMOID AND FLUTED POINTS FROM THE TRI-STATE AREA

State	County and Township	Locus	Terrain	Material	Length	Base	Widest Point	Fluting	Grinding	No.	Owner
Indiana	Dearborn	Laughery Creek (approx.)	valley near small creek	unknown	3-3/4"	1-5/16"	1-5/16"	3/4" one side; 1" the other.	base and 3/4"; 1" both edges.	17.	Mr. A. Behrman, Cincinnati
Kentucky	Boone	near Hamilton	unknown	black weathered flint	3-7/8"	7/16	1-1/16"	2-3/16" both sides	base and 5/8" on one edge; 3/4" on other edge.	18.	Robert Moody, Union, Ky.
Kentucky	Boone	below Camp Ernest on Gunpowder Creek.	low, narrow balley.	buff grey, shiny flint	2-3/4"	?	1"	1" both sides	base only	19.	Behringer Museum, Covington, Kentucky
Kentucky	Boone	near Union, Kentucky	upland eroded tableland	light brown fairly hard flint	2-1/2"	1-1/8"	1"	1-1/4" one side; 1-1/8" on other side.	base 1-1/4" on both edges.	20.	Robert Moody, Union, Ky.
Kentucky	Boone	around Union in Frogtown Rd. area	high eroded uplands	nearly white grainy, slightly weathered chert	2-1/2"	1"	1-3/16"	1-1/8" one side; 5/8" the other side	base and 1-1/4" one edge; 1,1/8" the other	21.	Mr. Gene Schlosser, Cincinnati
Kentucky	Campbell	on hill above steelmill on route	hilltop, overlooking short, flat valley	shiny, dark grey flint	2-1/2"	?	7/8"	1-7/8" on both sides.	?	22.	Behringer Museum, Covington, Kentucky

high and about 400 feet in circumference, enclosing a tumulus about four feet high; the material of which the embankment is formed, seems to have been taken from within the enclosure, forming an internal ditch — the other work is similar in character. Dec. 3, 1878." (2)

In the area of the Madisonville site (33-Ha.-36) were three more "sacred circles." All three were located on the Mariemont terrace, but cannot be considered as a group since they are located from one-half to one-quarter mile from each other. On the eastern side of the same terrace in section 9 stood a circular embankment, (33-Ha.-146) which was described by Mr. Florien Giauque, a Cincinnati attorney, in an 1876 periodical: (3)

"On the top of this ridge, there is a circular enclosure, made by a ditch, and an earthen embankment outside of and immediately adjoining this ditch, and no doubt made of the material which was taken from it. From the bottom of this ditch to the top of the embankment, the present height is about 5½'; the diameter of the ditch from deepest cut on either side is 75'; the enclosing embankment, from crest to crest, is 105'; and the diameter of the entire work from outside to outside is about 145'-150'. On the east, this embankment is enlarged into a regular mound, about 48' in diameter and about 6' high above the adjacent ground. At the S.E. part of the enclosure, there is left an entrance way about 10' wide — that is, there is here neither ditch nor embankment — this entrance faces and is about 40' away from the edge of the terrace or bluff, which is here quite steep."

The Mound located on the embankment rather than in the center is unusual and possibly unique. Mr. Giauque found a low limestone "arch", evidence of fire and two burials. It seems probable that this mound was a later addition to the enclosure.

A quarter mile N.N.W. from 33-Ha.-146, at the junction of Wooster and Plainville Pikes, stood an enclosure described by Metz. (33-Ha.-159) Its diameter was one hundred and ninety-one feet, and its central mound had an elevation of four feet. Many old residents of the area recall seeing this enclosure when paying the toll at the toll house which formerly stood on the ground where the small park is now located.

West from the above site and across Whiskey Run from the Madisonville Site (33-Ha.-36) is located the third Adena Circle on the plain of Mariemont (33-Ha.-152). It stands directly behind the old Joseph Ferris homestead on Wooster Pike and is sixty-five feet in diameter. The ditch was on the inside of the embankment and a small mound once stood in the center. Although both contours and original outward appearance are now

---

(2) In Metz, 1878. Cincinnati Museum of Natural History Library.

(3) Giauque, Florien, in *Harvest Home Magazine*, August, 1876.

completely obliterated, the sub-surface zone on the entire site is still undisturbed. Therefore, a careful excavation might reveal the post-mold pattern which one would expect to exist there.

The final Adena "sacred circle" in Columbia Township was located on the level terrace north of the Beechmont Levee and east of the Pennsylvania R.R. tracks. Although destroyed in the early 1870's, this site (33-Ha.-168) was adequately recorded in Dr. Metz's records. The central mound was originally eight feet high. In it were found two circular layers of human remains; one on the floor and the second three feet above the first. This burial arrangement is reminiscent of Greenman's mound, number fifty-seven and is heretofore unknown in the area. A further peculiarity of this site is that Metz gave the diameter of the circular enclosure as eight hundred feet, which is not only three hundred feet larger than the largest Sacred Circle mentioned by Webb and Snow, but much larger than the generally small circles in this area. It seems possible that since Metz usually gives only the circumference of circular works, that he might have meant that the circumference was eight hundred feet, which would make the diameter about two hundred and fifty-five feet which is the typical size of an Adena Circle. If an actual error in measurement existed here it could be due to the fact that most of the earthwork was obliterated by the time of Metz's survey.

In contrast to the large size of the preceding site, 33-Ha.-165 is only fifty feet in diameter. It is situated on a high hilltop about a mile south of the Dry Ridge Catholic Church in Colerain Township. It seems to be similar to the one recently discovered in the Girl Scout Camp in Butler County which is only a circular depression, forty-five feet in diameter. Like 33-Ha.-165, the Butler County enclosure is on high ground. When the survey visited it, charcoal was observed in the depression.

The village of Crescentville in Springfield Township is named for an earthwork (33-Ha.-206) which stood near the county line in the lowland between the old Miami and Erie Canal bed and the creek to the east. Mills, relying on the town's name, classified the site as a crescent. The last section of the embankment remaining was that segment farthest from the creek. The 1956 series of Department of Agriculture aerial photographs failed to show the site. We do not know of any so-called crescents which have been observed in anything but a state of near obliteration, and are inclined to classify this as a partially obliterated Adena circle.

Typical Adena Circles once existed in both Sayler Park (33-Ha.-158) and on E. Fifth Street in downtown Cincinnati (33-Ha.-222). Of the latter, Robert Clarke wrote:

> "On Fifth Street, to the East of Broadway, . . . , was a circular bank enclosing a space 60' in diameter, formed by throwing up the earth from the inside. It was not more than a foot in height, but twelve to fifteen feet wide.[1]

---

[1] Clark, Robert, *The Pre-historic Remains in the Site of the City of Cincinnati with a Vindication of the Cincinnati Tablet.* Cincinnati, 1876; p. 6.

At the S.E. end of the long, low ridge which once stood S.W. of the junction of Broadwell and Mt. Carmel Road in Anderson Township was an Adena circle with a central mound, which was known to Dr. Metz. (33-Ha.-44)[2] On the southeast side of the circle was a gateway fifty feet wide, over which the inner ditch was interrupted. Metz's thirty foot-wide trench through the low, elliptical central mound produced nothing more than a foot-thick layer of hard packed ashes and a lone pottery bead. It was still visible on aerial photographs as recently as 1956, but has since been totally destroyed by the Ohio Gravel Company. Unfortunately, no observers were present at the time of its destruction. A worker for the Ohio Gravel Company recalls finding "skeletons" in or near the site when it was destroyed.

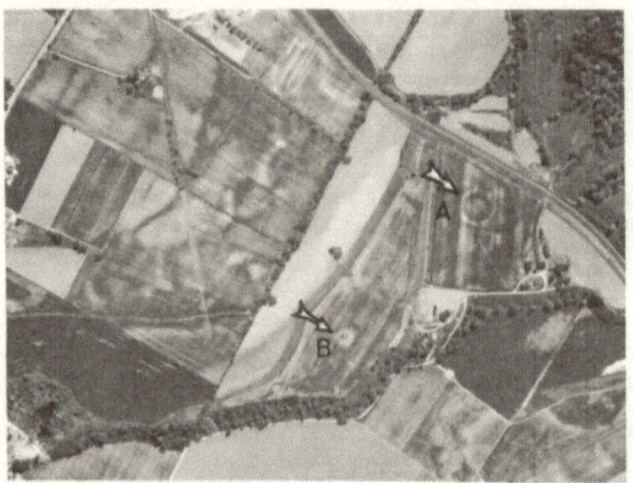

Aerial Photograph of: A) Circular Work (33-Ha-44); B) Mound
Anderson Township

In Section 21, Sycamore Township, on the hills east of Reading was a circle with an inner ditch and a central mound (33-Ha.-241). As in the case of the Ferris Earthwork, certain features of this enclosure may still exist and should be more fully explored. Mr. J. G. Olden stated that it stood on the old Price Thompson Farm.[3]

On the high ground south of Newtown was an Adena circle of which practically nothing is known today. It stood somewhere on the level terrace west of Newtown Road. On the northeast side of the wall was a small gateway. Another circle was situated near the junction of Batavia Pike and Little Dry Run Road on the old Abner Hahn farm. In recent years the entire property has been removed for gravel and all details of the earthwork have been permanently lost. Knowledge of both of these enclosures is based on an unsigned sketch map in the Peabody Museum, presumably made by a local resident (possibly Dr. Metz) before the turn of the century.

---

[2] Metz, Dr. Charles L., Unpublished notes. Peabody Museum, Cambridge, Massachusetts.

[3] Olden, J. G., *Reminiscences of Lockland and Reading*. Cincinnati, 1879; p. 16.

ADENA or "SACRED" CIRCLES in HAMILTON COUNTY, OHIO

Site Number	Township	Diameter	Central Mound	Topography Hill-top	Topography River Terrace	Topography Valley	Ditch Inside	Ditch Outside	Remarks
33–Ha.–222	downtown Cincinnati	90 ft.			X		X		Located East of Fountain Square on Fifth Street.
33–Ha.–44	Anderson	200 ft.	X		X		X		Partially explored by the Literary and Scientific Society of Madisonville in the 1870's. Had a 30' gateway on the southern side.
33–Ha.–241	Sycamore		X	X			X		Located in Section 21 on high ground.
33–Ha.–266	Anderson	170 ft.	X		X				The wall was interrupted by a gateway on the northeast side.
33–Ha.–267	Anderson		X			X			On the now destroyed Abner Hahn farm near Little Dry Run Road and Batavia Pike.

ADENA or "SACRED" CIRCLES in HAMILTON COUNTY, OHIO

Site Number	Township	Diameter	Central Mound	Topography			Ditch		Remarks
				Hill-top	River Terrace	Valley	Inside	Outside	
33-Ha.-166	Columbia	127 ft.	X	X			X		These two circles are located near and are probably associated with each other.
33-Ha.-167	Columbia	127 ft.	X	X			X		
33-Ha.-146	Columbia	145 ft.			X		X		Although these three circles all stand on the plateau of Mariemont, they are probably unrelated to one another.
33-Ha.-150	Columbia	191 ft.	X		X				
33-Ha.-152	Columbia	65 ft.	X		X		X		
33-Ha.-168	Columbia	800 ft.	X		X				Dr. Metz probably erred in giving the diameter as 800'. This was most likely the circumference, making a 255' diameter.
33-Ha.-165	Colerain	50 ft.		X					Unusual in that it is isolated from other archaeological sites on a high hilltop.
33-Ha.-206	Springfield	?				X			This was listed by Mills as a crescent. It was probably a partially obliterated Adena circle.
33-Ha.-158	Delhi	?			X				Possibly related to the Sayler Park Mound.

CEREMONIAL EARTHWORKS

Although Hopewellian earthworks do not occur as frequently in Hamilton County as they do in the Ross County area, the eight which once existed here are all interesting and in many respects unusual.

The first earthwork to attract attention was the one situated near present Fountain Square in Downtown Cincinnati (33-Ha.-778). Dr. Daniel Drake is the only early author to make mention of this work. His description is complete and detailed. The structure was in the form of a large oval which extended from the west side of Race Street nearly to Walnut and from slightly above Fifth Street to a few feet south of Fourth Street. From the gateway on the east, a segment ran due south toward the river and turned east at a point above Third Street, paralleling that street to Main, where it terminated in a mound (33-Ha.-227). Just north of the north side of the gateway, or near the corner of Sixth and Walnut were two low mounds (33-Ha.-230). Also, a segment of a large circle once extended from Sixth and Sycamore east to Broadway and on to Third and Sycamore (33-Ha.-229). Clarke reported that early settlers recalled seeing an embankment extending south from the mound (33-Ha.-227) to the River. Although Clarke doubted the early settlers' report, there is reason for believing it, for the famous Hopewell Works in Ross County were also constructed on two terraces with walls uninterrupted by the contour.

By a slow process of erosion and excavation, 33-Ha.-227 has been destroyed. Fortunately, Dr. Drake recorded the finds in his usual meticulous manner. Artifacts mentioned by him include five "plummets," a circular "ring figure made from cannel coal" with a deep groove in its outer edge, a carved head and beak of an eagle, a fragment of thin copper with two perforations, a thin copper tube, carved bone, galena, mica, beads, marine shells, and copper spools with "lint" around them. Nearly thirty burials in "rude coffins of stone," surrounded with ashes and charcoal were found when dirt was removed from the mound. An extended burial with the skull toward the west is also mentioned. Concerning the construction of the mound, Drake wrote:

> "The first artificial layer was of gravel, considerably raised in the middle; the next, composed of large pebbles, was convex, and of uniform thickness; the last consisted of loam and soil; these deposits were entire and must have been made after the deposits in the tumulus were completed."[1]

This mound was certainly built by the Hopewell people. The circular cannel coal object appears to be similar to an artifact found at the Turner Group. According to Dr. James B. Griffin, these cannel coal rings should be considered a Hopewellian trait.[2] The "carved bone" was later reproduced by W. Strickland. His drawing, however, differs in many details

---

[1] Drake, Dr. Daniel, *A Picture of Cincinnati*, Cincinnati, 1815.

[2] Griffin, Dr. James B., personal communications. See p. 61 of *The Turner Group of Earthworks*, Willoughby, 1922.

from the one which appeared in the American Philosophical Society's "Transactions". The only copy of the Strickland reproduction to come to our attention is in the library of The Cincinnati Museum of Natural History; in it the raptorial bird motif containing all of the five elements defined by Webb and Baby,[3] i.e., head, body, wing, foot and tail, is detectable. Copper spools with "lint" around them were probably not used as ear spools, but their existence in the mound lends more support to the theory of its Hopewell origin. Galena, mica, and marine shells are all objects relatively common in Hopewell manifestations. An interesting sidelight on these artifacts is that they were brought to the attention of both Joseph Priestley, the noted English chemical pioneer, and Benjamin Franklin.[4] That two of the most famous scientists of the day should take an interest in Hamilton County archaeology is indeed a lasting compliment both to the achievements of the Hopewell culture and to eighteenth century science.

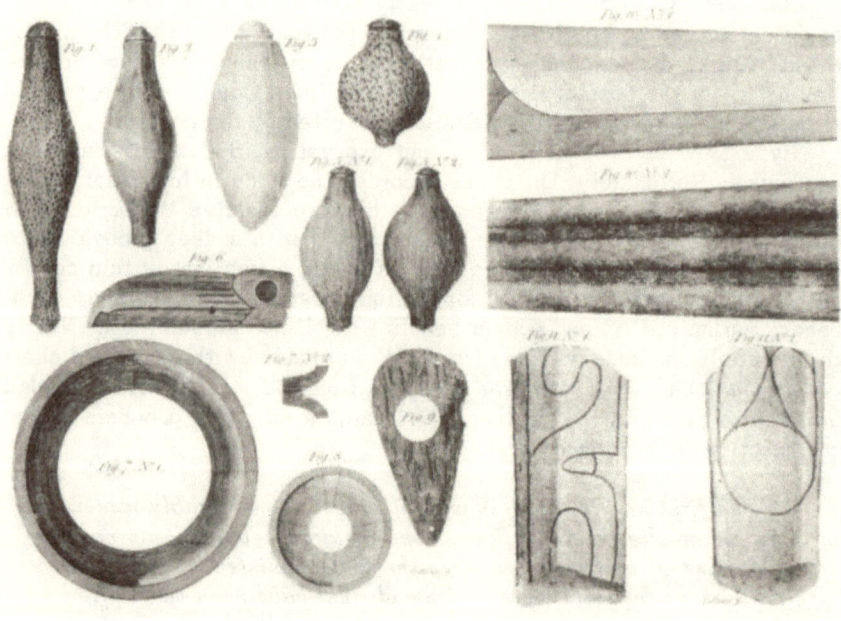

Artifacts from Third Street Mound (33-Ha-227)
(American Philosophical Society)

---

[3] Webb and Baby, *The Adena People 2*, Ohio State University Press, Columbus, 1957; p. 89.

[4] *Transactions*, The American Philosophical Society, 1780-1820. Philadelphia.

Another enclosure is located in section 30 of Colerain Township (33-Ha.-237). The Great Miami at this point makes a broad bend as it flows through a wide, level plain. It was near this spot that Dunlap Station, a pioneer blockhouse, was built in the late eighteenth century. The prehistoric earthwork formed a broad elipse with its northern and southern ends terminating at the river's edge. The walls themselves were at one time nine feet high and enclosed an area of ninety-five acres. On the northeastern side of the wall a curious loop is formed by the embankment, but in other respects it is regular. This is one of the few sites within Hamilton County that Squire and Davis mentioned in their 1848 publication:

>"*This work is situated near the village of Colerain, Hamilton County, Ohio, on the right bank of the Great Miami River, and encloses an area of ninety-five acres. The walls have an average height of nine feet, and have an exterior ditch of proportionate dimensions. The upheaved gravel upon the exterior side of the wall, wherever it is under cultivation, supports dwarfed and sickly maize; while on the inner side the grain is luxuriant.*" (5)

After an unsuccessful attempt to locate the site on the ground, the Department of Agriculture's aerial photographs were checked. The outline of the earthwork was detectable by its lighter color, but the peculiar irregularity in the wall which is shown on the Squire and Davis plate number XIII, No. 2, does not appear on the photographs. The artifact-bearing level is now beneath at least two feet of silt, and the walls, instead of being completely obliterated by plowing and erosion, are in part, at least, covered over by the river loam. See photo next page.

In the Southeast corner of Anderson Township on the high hill east of Eight Mile Creek is located an earthwork which is still visible. (33-Ha.-104) The work consists of two mounds in an east-west line from which low parallel embankments thirty yards long extend to the southwest. The westernmost wall makes an abrupt right angle turn and connects with the eastern wall which continues southwest to the edge of the steep hill. The mounds are of similar size and shape, three feet high and thirty feet in diameter. The eastern mound has been trenched by artifact collectors. An examination of the eroding trench showed no loading or other features. Although there are many mounds of stone and old roads in this area which are remnants of pioneer farmers, the inaccessibility of the hilltop and the poor soil conditions preclude a historic origin for the earthwork. On the level terrace below the crest

---

(5) Squire and Davis, *Ancient Monuments of the Mississippi Valley*, Reports of the Smithsonian Institute, p. 35.

[1] Metz, Dr. Charles, *Prehistoric Monuments of Anderson Township*, Cincinnati Museum of Natural History Journal, p. 304.

Colerain Works, Colerain Twp. from Squier & Davis' Ancient Monuments of the Mississippi Valley

of the hill and directly to the west of 33-Ha.-104 is the site of a cemetery mentioned by Metz.[1] The level bluff on which the cemetery is located is just north of River Road at Eight Mile Creek. Prior to 1880, extended burials were found there. (33-Ha.-188).

Another non-geometric earthwork is situated in present-day Terrace Park (33-Ha.-202).

Camden Works - Terrace Park - 33-Ha.-202
Little Miami River at Bottom and Right

> "Number 6 of this Group is a small mound, situated in section 22, Columbia Township, on an elevated ridge known as Gravelotte, on the estate of P.R. Biggs. It is situated in a corner of a large embankment. Its height is 3 feet, circumference 150 feet... In the southeast corner of Section 29, at the village of Camden and 300 feet east of the south line of Mr. Galloway's residence, is the corner of an embankment which extends east and south to the river. It extends ¾ of a mile east, until it reaches the bank of the river, which is here about 40 feet high, the other running south until it reaches the edge of the gravel ridge, and then runs east to the river. It encloses from 800 to 1000 acres of ground. This embankment, 50 years ago, was 6 feet high and 12 feet wide. It is now scarcely traceable, and is best discoverable in springtime, and just after plowing, when it can be readily traced across the fields by the peculiar color of the soil."[6]

The western wall of this earthwork or fortification parallels the Pennsylvania Railroad tracks in the old Robinson Circus grounds. The mound in the southwestern corner of the enclosure was not destroyed until 1957. Although many of the older local amateur archaeologists are familiar with this mound, neither they nor local folk could furnish any information about the enclosure. Instead, the mention of archaeology to the oldtimers usually brings to their minds the story of the renowned burial of Tillie, a circus elephant, who was interred near the mound after she had been killed in a nearby train wreck. The Terrace Park plain is admirably suited to both defensive and occupational needs. It is similar in character to the Mariemont Terrace. The unusual size of this work and the dearth of artifacts from the area make this site interesting and unique.

Near the corner of the Mt. Carmel Road and Round Bottom Road in Anderson Township, is one of the most dense concentrations of Hopewellian sites in this part of Ohio. The many mounds and village sites all center around the Turner Works (33-Ha.-41). The first mention of this work was in 1850 by Whittlesey. His drawing of the site contained many errors which were not recognized until the 1880's. The detailed excavation was conducted by Dr. Charles L. Metz of Madisonville, who worked under the auspices of the Peabody Museum of Harvard University. Although an apparently complete campaign of excavation was carried on from May, 1882, until 1908, many mounds in and around the work are still visible, and should attract further excavation. As it originally existed, the Turner Group consisted of an Elevated Circle five hundred and forty feet in diameter, from which it extended a Graded Way leading east to the elliptical Great Enclosure, which enclosed a large area on the lower plain. To the north and to the south of the

---

[6] Metz, Dr. Charles L., *The Prehistoric Monuments of the Little Miami Valley*, Cincinnati Museum of Natural History Journal, 1878, p. 9.

Elevated Circle were two triangular-shaped elevations, separated from the circle by ditches 20 feet in depth. Within the Elevated Circle were two mounds, and within the Great Enclosure were ten mounds. In addition to the mounds in the Great Enclosure, there were two small circular earthworks, three hundred and fifty and one hundred and forty feet in diameter, respectively.

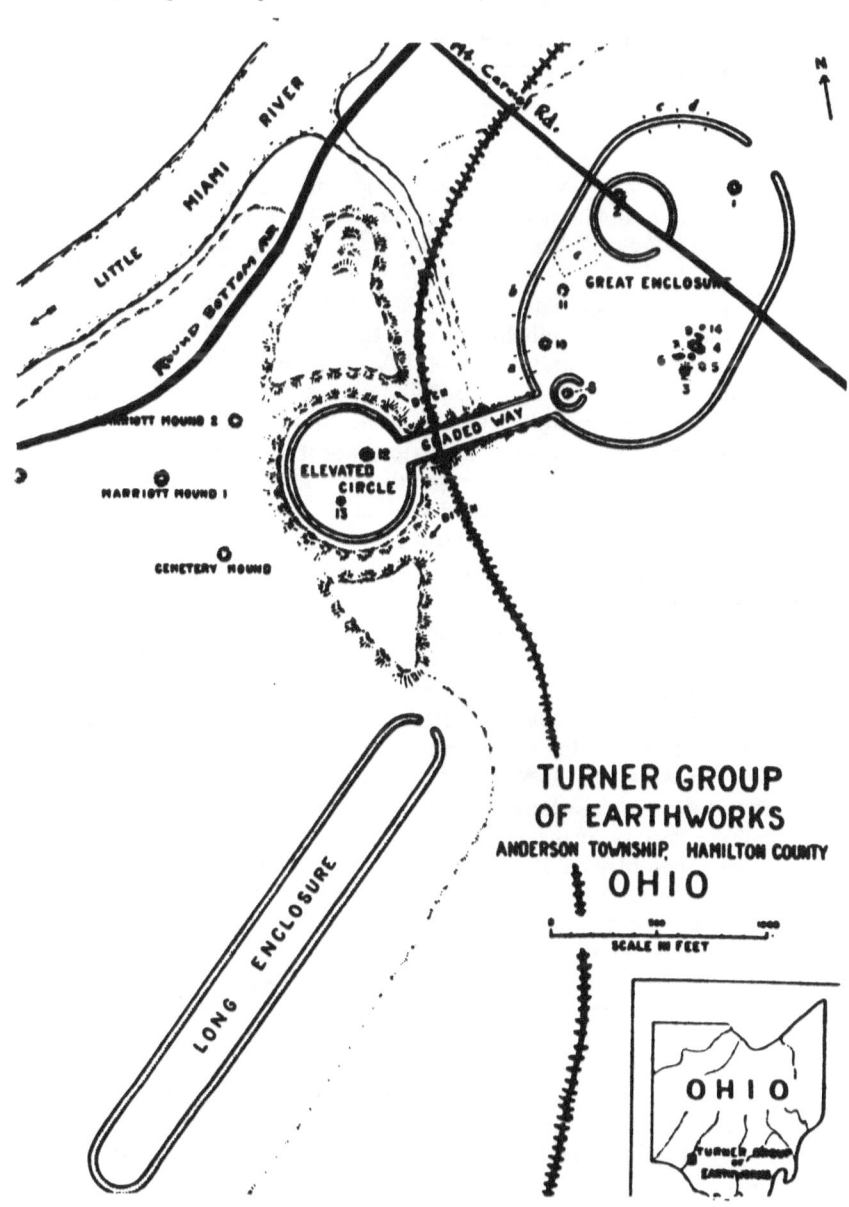

The Turner Group, Anderson Township
(D. S. & J. A. Hosbrook)

At the time of Dr. Metz's excavation, the southeastern section of the embankment around the Great Enclosure was nearly obliterated. However, the Graded Way, Elevated Circle, and the mounds within the two were all prominent. To the west of the Elevated Circle, and just outside of the deep ditches, were three mounds, the Marriott Mounds #1 and #2, and the Cemetery Mound. West of these was another small mound. Still another pebble-covered mound was located upon the river bank, and nine hundred feet north of the Great Enclosure (33-Ha.-179).

Of the parallel walls near the Turner Works (33-Ha.-177), Willoughby wrote,

> *"Eight hundred feet south from the Elevated Circle is the entrance to the long enclosure, with low parallel embankments and rounded ends. This is nearly one-half mile in length and about 250 feet in width."*(7)

These parallel walls are not visible, but Willoughby's description indicates that they were probably similar to those at Ft. Ancient and the ones in downtown Cincinnati (33-Ha.-223). The ones in Cincinnati stood between Vine and Elm Streets, Central Parkway and 12th Streets. Although they were destroyed before 1830, Dr. Drake's description reveals that they were smaller in every dimension than those at the Turner Site. Their length was seven hundred and sixty feet, and with the exception of the ends, they were parallel. Toward the end of each wall, they narrowed to forty feet apart. An opening, thirty feet wide, was near the southern end of the southern wall; with the exception of this opening, the walls were uninterrupted.

The Peabody Museum's excavation proved the Turner Site to be one of the most sensational of large Hopewellian earthworks. Although the excavation was inadequate in the recordings of house patterns and other structural features, numerous artifacts of inestimable artistic value were found, and sections of the work were explored which have since been destroyed. On Altar #1, in Mound #4 (within the Great Enclosure) fragments of terra cotta figurines were found, which far surpass the usual crude representations of the human form found in most eastern American sites. Their importance lies both in their artistic merit and also in their informative nature, for they not only show dress and hair styles, but also indicate the physical appearance of the Hopewellian folk.

Possibly even more important is the large effigy of a lizard-like monster carved from a rudy slate. (See Frontispiece) Two bent horns emerge from the reptile-like head and rattlesnake rattles compose the tail. In addition to the four legs, carved in low relief on the sides of the body, are bands of cross-hatched engravings which ornament the back. That the figure had some functional role is suggested by the dish-like hollow in the under side. Suggestions of further decoration survive in the tooth holes, in which were probably inserted small animal

---

(7)Willoughby, Charles C., *The Turner Group of Earthworks*, Peabody Museum of Archaeology and Ethnology, Vol. VIII, No. 3, 1922, p. 5.

Seated Figure — Terra-Cotta
Turner Works
(Peabody Museum, Cambridge)

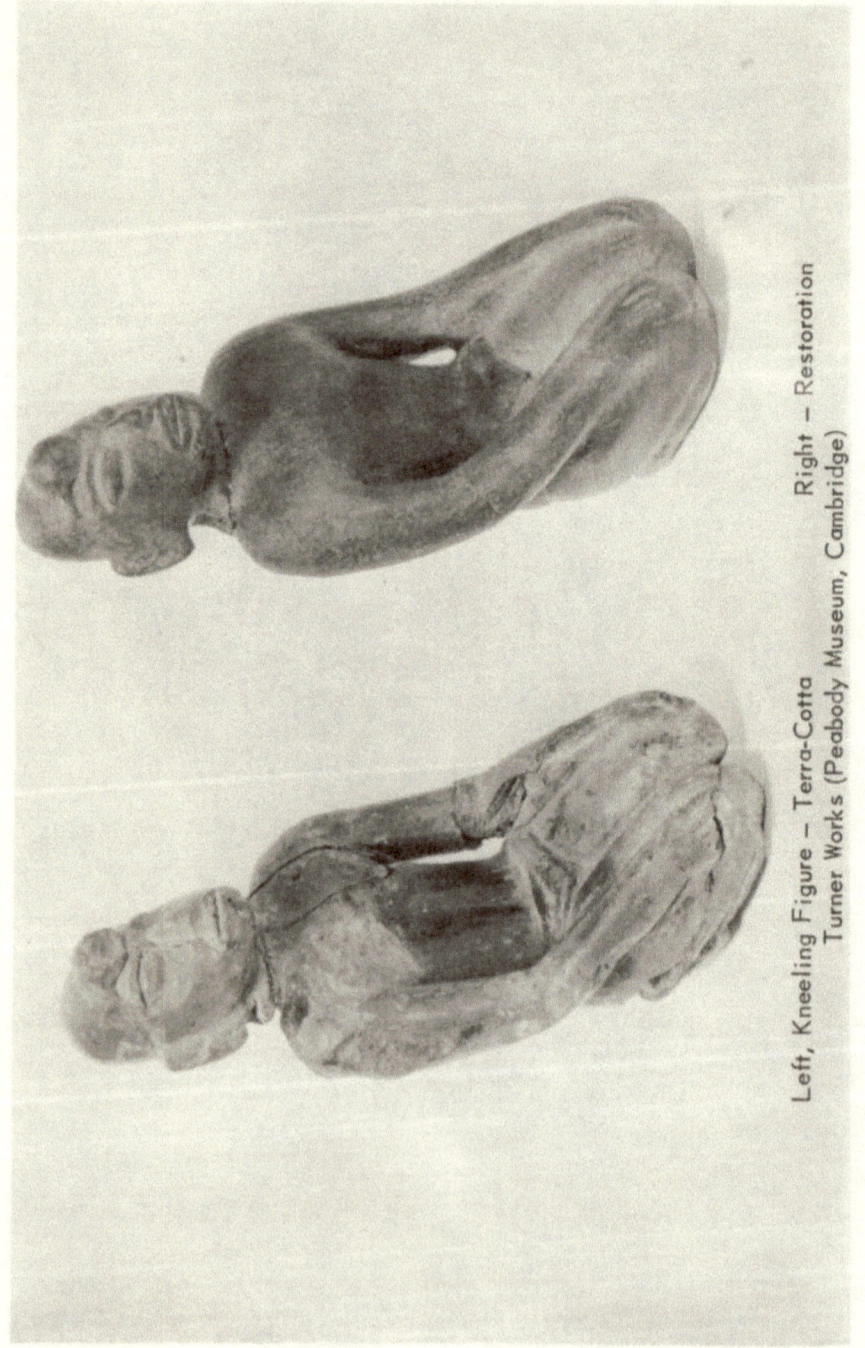

Left, Kneeling Figure – Terra-Cotta   Right – Restoration
Turner Works (Peabody Museum, Cambridge)

Male Figure — Terra-Cotta
Mound 4, Turner Group
(Peabody Museum, Cambridge)

Right, Female Figure — Terra-Cotta.   Left — Restoration
Mound 4, Turner Works
(Peabody Museum, Cambridge)

teeth, and the hollow, circular eye holes, where some stone, metal or pearl spheres were once placed. This effigy and the human figurines, comprise what is probably the single most important sculptured find from the North American continent.

The Survey's collection, from the Turner Works itself, consist of the following artifacts:

> numerous hammerstones
> one mortar
> one Harrison County flint flake knife
> numerous cores
> one finely worked celt from the Elevated Circle

This collection was made in those areas of the site which still remain, namely, the Elevated Circle, the deep ditches surrounding it, the triangular elevations to the north and south of the Elevated Circle, and the first ten feet of the Graded Way. Within the Elevated Circle, Mounds #12 and #13 are still visible. As far as can be ascertained, the bases and subsoil of the mounds have not as yet been excavated. Number 12, the larger of the two, was fifty-two feet in diameter, and over five feet high. A circular wall was, according to Dr. Metz, thirty-four inches high and resting on a four-inch layer of gravel. In and around the mound numerous burials were found. A slight cavity in the very center of the mound produced one unio shell, but the descriptions and drawings in the Peabody Report indicate that the entire subfloor area was not excavated.

Of mound number 13, Willoughby wrote:

> *"This is the smaller of the two mounds in the elevated circle. It was approximately 30 feet in diameter, and 2 feet high. Upon removing the earth, a circular pavement of flat river stones, 15 feet in diameter, was found. This rested on a layer of sand, 8 inches deep. The clay beneath the sand showed no evidence of having been disturbed."*[8]

The Ohio Gravel Company, which now owns the Turner Site, is just finishing the final destruction of it for the valuable gravel which underlies the entire area. In addition to the site itself, numerous other mounds and village sites have been affected. Among them are the Marriott Mounds mentioned earlier which are both within the areas being explored. Marriott Mound #1 was a low pebble-covered mound, two feet high and sixty feet in diameter. From Willoughby's description, it seems possible that this mound and the other pebble-covered mound on the river bank (33-Ha.-179) were of a similar nature. The excavation uncovered a low altar, six burials, a "plate" of native copper, copper ear ornaments, perforated bear teeth inlaid with large pearls, pearl beads, and other

---

[8] Willoughby, Charles C. *The Turner Group of Earthworks*, p. 85.

artifacts. One of the "ear spools" was wound with cord, much like the one found in 33-Ha.-227, mentioned earlier. The remaining fragment of of this mound is still readily visible in Mr. Denneman's cornfield. (33-Ha.-54)

Marriott Mound #2 (33-Ha.-178), four hundred feet N.E. of 33-Ha.-54, was also excavated by Metz and Putnam in 1884. Although it was said to be "of little interest,"[9] it is still visible and should be re-excavated before it is destroyed completely.

A short distance southwest from Marriott Mound #2 is located the Cemetery Mound (33-Ha.-52), the old graveyard of the pioneer Marriott family. The diameter of this mound is thirty yards, its height three feet; the numerous recent graves have slightly reduced the height and have probably disturbed the contents of the mound. It is ironical that, of all the mounds in and around the Turner Works, only this one, which is probably of the least archaeological value, will be preserved. See photos the following pages.

DEFENSIVE FORTIFICATIONS

Within Hamilton County there are three earth-walled fortifications. In size they are rivalled only by the geometric earthworks of the Hopewell Culture. The most important is the famous Miami Fort (33-Ha.-62) on the high hills at the confluence of the Ohio and the Great Miami Rivers. Practically every local antiquarian from Andrew Porter in 1802 until the present has made some mention of it and the many sites around it. The fort itself is rather small, enclosing about 12 acres along the tops of two hills. The level table land in the center of the earthwork is ten to twenty feet above the walls themselves, which are on the sides of the hill. The embankments vary from one to twelve feet in height and are interrupted by many gateways, some intentionally constructed, and others caused by erosion. In certain sections of the north wall, recent erosion has laid bare an underlying layer of hard clay burnt to a bright orange. Another example of this type of construction occurs at the Clark's Works, a fort at Fosters, Ohio, in Warren County.[1] Other points of similarity between these widely separated forts are the low stone retaining walls found at the outer base of the embankment at both sites. Miami Fort is covered with a dense growth of forest trees with the exception of the Northeast corner, where erosion is fast becoming a major problem. In other eroded areas within the fort, village material has been found from time to time, and stone graves, similar to those at Fort Ancient, have been found on the precipitous hillside immediately outside the walls. A rectangular slate gorget was recently found with a burial in one of these graves. A mound on the westermost corner of the earthwork makes a prominent lookout into the valley below. Fortunately, Miami Fort, or Fort Hill, as it is variously called, is a Cincinnati park and may some day get the attention and preservation it deserves.

---

[9] *Ibid.*, p. 88.

[1] Fowke, Gerard, *Archaeological History of Ohio*, Columbus, 1902, p. 256.

Utilitarian Ware,
Turner Group, Anderson Township
(Peabody Museum, Cambridge)

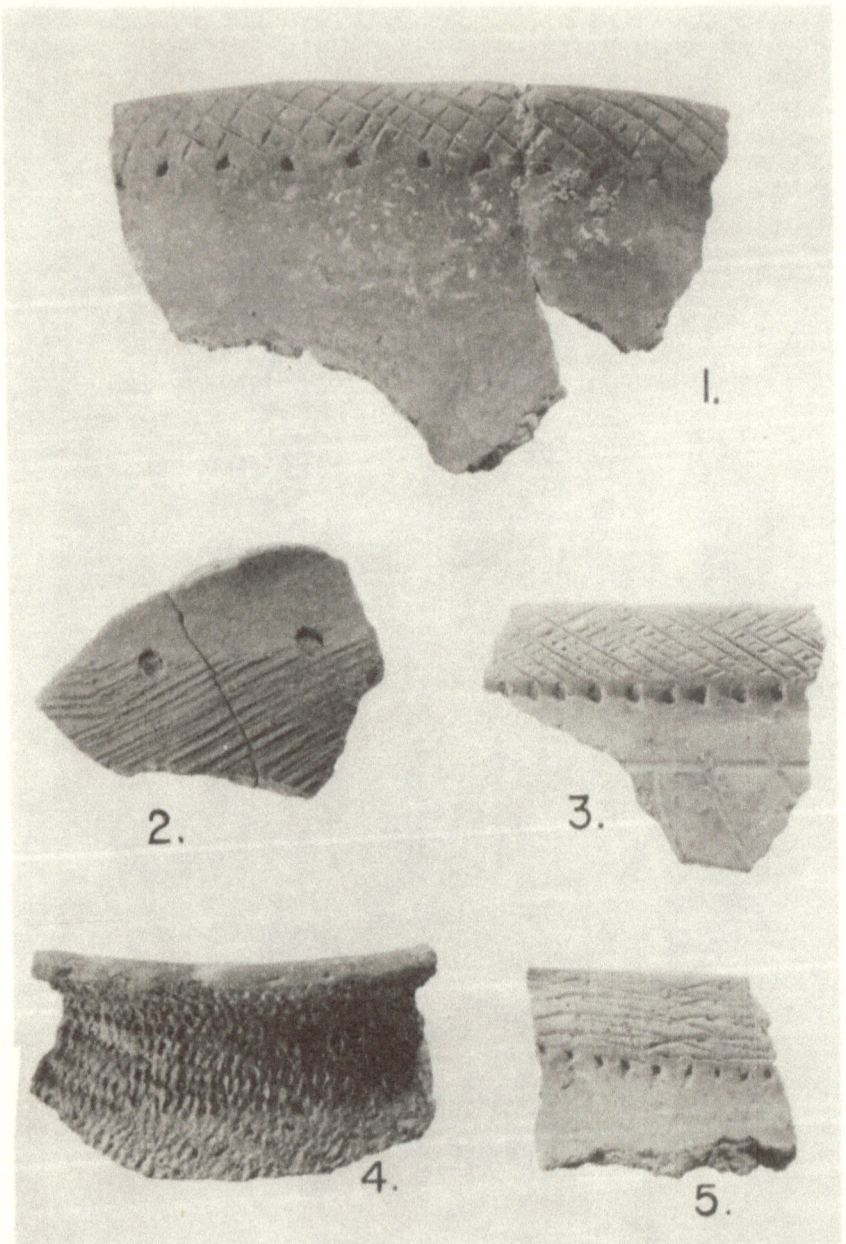

Pot Sherds from the Turner Works, Anderson Township

1. Rim sherd, grit tempered from Ash bed embankment.
2. Fine sand tempered brushed ware; from embankment.
3. Rim sherd, limestone tempered. Mound #3.
4. Rim sherd, grit tempered cord impressed. Mound #3.
5. Plain Rocker stamped rim sherd. Clay tempered. Pit #1.

Pot Sherds from the Turner Group, Anderson Township
1. Limestone tempered, cambered rim. Mound #4.
2. Cord Marked rim sherd with cord impressions on lip. Mound #4.
3. Fine Sand Tempered rim sherd.
4. Limestone tempered rim sherd with incised design. Marriott Mound #1.
5. Limestone tempered plain rim sherd.

Pot Sherds from the Turner Works, Anderson Township
1. Brushed, sand tempered ware. Mound #1.
2. Dentate Rocker stamped, limestone tempered ware. Mound #3.
3. Rocker stamped, possibly zoned ware. From Ash Bed.
4. Plain Rocker stamped ware. Limestone and grit tempered. Mound #3.
5. Plain Rocker Stamped Ware. Limestone tempered from Trench II.

Grit Tempered Stamped Ware
Turner Works
(Peabody Museum, Cambridge)

Miami Fort, Miami Township (Squier & Davis)

On the long hilltop northeast of the Sand Ridge village site (33-Ha.-17) is located a second fortification (33-Ha.-216). The earth walls vary in height from one to three and one-half feet and, like most hilltop fortifications, the embankment is slightly below the brow of the hill. Springs abound in the area, and Woodland village material occurs in various places within the fort. Just southwest of the enclosure is a small village site (33-Ha.-70) at which the following material was found:

> two hafted scrapers
> two limestone tempered cordmarked sherds
> two broken projectile points
> numerous flakes
> fire-cracked rock

The pottery is similar to that found on the Woodland level of Sand Ridge, the Turpin Farm, and many other stratified sites in the Little Miami valley. Within the walls of the fort and on the highest point immediately above 33-Ha.-17 was once a small circle of standing stones. Dr. Metz stated that the circle was ten feet in diameter and composed of stones from ten to twelve inches thick and four to five feet long. Mr. Phillip Nunn, who now owns part of the Sand Ridge, recalls seeing this circle and has confirmed Dr. Metz's figures. Both the earthwork and the circle have been obliterated by recent clearing in preparation for building.

On the edge of the Mariemont bluff, extending east from the large Madisonville site (33-Ha.-36) for nearly two hundred and fifty yards, is a pronounced earthwork (33-Ha.-37). Its height varies from a few inches to about four feet. Very few residents of the area are aware of the antiquity of this work. However, Messrs. Hack and Ward, lifelong residents of Madisonville, both remember seeing the embankment as it now is, over fifty years ago. No record exists of other embankments in Mariemont which might have fortified the north side of the terrace.

STONE MOUNDS

Of the approximately twenty stone mounds which once stood in the county, all but six have been destroyed or excavated. About eight of the destroyed mounds were excavated, most of them in the 1870's, but one in the 1940's. The first excavation of a local stone mound was that conducted by Dr. H. H. Hill in 1874 (33-Ha.-156). It was located on the highest point of land above Fairview Park, and commanded a lovely view of the plain of Cincinnati. The H. H. Hill Mound contained most of the salient "Stone Mound" traits. Dr. Hill

> "... found that the remains were distributed over a circular space of about forty feet in diameter, on the extreme point of the hill, with the ground sloping in every direction. The few human bones found were so much decayed that they crumbled

> to powder on exposure. Most of them were quite near the surface, but may have been covered four or five feet with the stones which had been taken away from the place. This, however, could not be definitely determined. Some appeared to have been buried in a sitting position, as the teeth were found near the thigh bones..."[1]

Besides human teeth, a large number of animal teeth and tusks were found with fragments of deer horn, bone awls, and bone awl-cases. The latter were made by splitting the lower leg bone of elk or buffalo, straightening out the edges, and scraping out the inside so that, when bound together, they formed a case. Some of them contained bone awls, or needles, when found, but all were more or less broken. There were also pieces of mica, hammerstones and gorgets, three stone pipes, flint spears and arrowheads, some copper awls, fragments of shells, on one of which were traces of a carving.

In the early 1880's, Dr. Metz excavated the Edwards Stone Mound (33-Ha.-205). It was located in the level bottom land adjoining the Little Miami River west of Round Bottom Road and three-fifths of a mile southwest of Benchmark 513. In a letter dated March, 1883, to Professor F.W. Putnam of Harvard University, Dr. Metz described the mound:

> "At the time when I was engaged in the exploration of the large Edwards Mound No. 22, Mr. Edwards called my attention to a mound situated on the higher portion of the first bottom of the Little Miami River, and on a direct line N.W. from mound No. 22 distant about 500 yards from it. On visiting the locality with Mr. Edwards, I found the mound located about 100 yards from the river bank, on the higher portion of the plain, which is here elevated about 25 feet above low water mark of the river, and is not subject to inundation except at unusually high freshets of the river. The mound appeared about 2½ feet high, 100 feet in diameter N. & S. and measured 120 feet in length E. & W. Mr. Edwards informed me that 60 years ago the mound was between 8 and 9 feet high, and was covered with the forest that also occupied all of the surrounding plain. Shortly after this time the land was cleared, and he himself scraped down part of the mound, requiring the earth to fill up a depression in the plain nearby. He removed about 4 feet of the earth from the top when he encountered stones and human remains, for 50 years past he has cultivated the mound annually, and during the period has removed quantities of stone from it, besides ploughing up many skeletons and other bones, however finding no relics.

---

[1] Clarke, Robert, Op. cit., p. 15.

"On March 8, we began exploration of the mound by making an excavation 15 ft. wide at the edge of the mound on the N.E. At a depth of 8 inches a layer of stone was found which extended upwards conforming to the slope of the sides of the mound. This stone was found to consist of from 4 to 7 courses being heavier in some places than in others and subsequently proved to extend entirely around the sides of the mound. The stones were of all sizes, from that not larger than a man's hand to that which can hardly be lifted. The larger stones were the hill limestones and were brought from the hills ¾ mile distant while the smaller were flat and water worn, and evidently were taken from the river and drift gravel beds nearby. They were disposed in regular layers, some care seems to have been taken in their arrangements, this was evident wherever we found them undisturbed. Near the surface of the mound, many fragments of human and animal remains were found intermingled with stones that had been torn up by the plough. The men were instructed to completely uncover the stones all around the base. After this was done, a trench 25 ft. wide was begun on the N.E. side, and was carried through the centre of the mound. About 2 ft. from the edge of the mound a skeleton was discovered...

On the south side of the mound was a space 10 ft. wide and 12 ft. long where a fire had been kept up for some length of time, as the earth was burned red to a depth of 2 or 3 inches. In this space almost all of the animal remains and fragments of pottery sent you were obtained. Here was also found a considerable quantity of burned Unio shells. Five were found buried over this space, seemingly some time after the burning over this space. The base of the mound formed a complete circle 270 ft. around and 90 ft. in diameter..."(2)

The seventy-one burials in the mound can be broken down as follows:

    32 extended — 17 with artifacts in association
    22 flexed — 6 with artifacts in association
    5 in one heap
    1 child
    1 with skull associated
    2 isolated skulls
    8 fragmentary

In many instances, the hands of the extended burials were either over the body to the skull or to the pelvis. Of the extended burials, three had large, upright, stone slabs near the head or feet. The skeleton of a "dog or young bear" was found near an extended burial. The artifacts collected from the burials include:

---

(2)Metz, Dr. Charles L., Unpublished letter. Peabody Museum, Cambridge, Mass.

2 shell ornaments
1 drill
9 projectile points
potsherds
14 bone awls
3 copper awls
3 bone beads
1 bone gorget
5 bear teeth
4 cut bear teeth
1 beaver's tooth
4 turtle shells
1 tooth pendant
1 bone tube
3 celts
worked bone

Surrounding the mound is a village site which is also designated 33-Ha.-42. Even from a superficial glance it is evident that the pottery from the village is identical to that found in the mound.

1 re-worked polished celt
1 unpolished celt
2 cores
x flakes
1 scraper
2 stemmed projectile points
3 side notched projectile points
1 corner notched projectile point
3 broken projectile points
3 grit-tempered cordmarked sherds
3 grit-tempered plain sherds
3 limestone-tempered plain sherds
2 limestone-tempered, cordmarked sherds
broken rock

The above material was all found in 1957; the site has not yielded any artifacts since then.

In front of the old Philip Turpin home on the Batavia Pike in Anderson Township was located a low stone mound (33-Ha.-160) which was excavated in 1949 by the Cincinnati Museum of Natural History. Unlike most stone mounds, this one was located on the edge of a low terrace in the river bottoms. Both extended and flexed burials were found. The original appearance of the mound's surface and contents had been greatly modified by the later Fort Ancient intrusions.

On the high hilltop behind Hooven, Ohio, in Whitewater Township are located two stone mounds (33-Ha.-248). Both of these mounds have been dug into, but substantial parts of both still exist. From this hilltop, which separates the valley of the Miami from that of the Whitewater, an extensive view spreads out in every direction.

On the spine of the hill overlooking Muddy Creek, in Sayler Park, is a small stone mound (33-Ha.-27). Although only sixteen feet in diameter, it is nevertheless notable for its location. Instead of being built on a hilltop, it was constructed on the sloping spine of the ridge.

To the southwest of Miami Fort is a point of land connected to it by a narrow isthmus. Looking out from "the point" one has a magnificent view of the junction of the Great Miami and Ohio Rivers. Near the fort on this point of land is a five foot-high earth mound, while on the tip stands a stone mound (33-Ha.-63). Its height was once two and one-half feet, but, as in the case of the Fairview Park mound, its diameter could not be determined due to the sloping hillside. Uncremated human bones have recently been found here by Boy Scouts who often camp in the fort and have caused considerable damage to the mound and to the beauty of this spot.

Three groups of other small stone mounds were opened by the Literary and Scientific Society of Madisonville in the 1880's. The first two groups were on hilltops in Symmes Township, one near Symmes Station, two others north of Loveland, and the last on the old Kendall farm near Madisonville. They were all of the single-grave type and all contained the bones in roughly-formed coffins of stones. Especially important is the group near Loveland because of the artifacts which were discovered in them. Atypical pieces were copper ear spools and a lancellate head similar to two specimens from the Edwin Harness Mound; more usual specimens include stemmed points and copper awls.[3] This type of small-scale mound, or better, cairn, seems to have been by far the most preferred type of stone burial in the County. It is interesting to note that whereas the more elaborate structures have been found on hilltops (Point Stone Mound), no cairns have been discovered to date in the bottoms.

The three final stone mounds in the county are all in Anderson Township. The Whetstone mound (33-Ha.-181) and the Dry Run Mound (33-Ha.-214) were both discovered by Dr. Metz and were designated No. 3, group F and No. 24, group C, respectively. Of 33-Ha.-181, Dr. Metz wrote:

> It is constructed of flat slabs of limestone of various sizes; the greater portion of the stones visible show evidence of the action of fire. It has an elevation of five and one half feet and a diameter at base of fifty feet.[4]

The mound is located on the high ridge exactly opposite the lake at Coney Island. Part of this mound still remains and local residents confirm Dr. Metz's report as to the evidence of fire. A butterfly bannerstone was found a few feet from this mound, and is now in the Behrman Collection.

33-Ha.-214 is located *"on a spur of land about one hundred and fifty feet above the level of Dry Run, about three hundred yards southeast of*

---

[3]Metz, Dr. Charles L., unpublished manuscripts, Peabody Museum, Cambridge, Massachusetts.

[4]*Op. cit.*, Metz, Dr. Charles L., 1881. p. 303

Stone Cairn "B" excavated by Dr. C. L. Metz, 1884.
Located near Loveland, Symmes Township.
(Photo by Dr. C. L. Metz, courtesy of Peabody Museum, Cambridge, Mass.)

Artifacts found by Dr. Metz in Stone Cairn, Loveland, Symmes Township
1. fragmentary copper awl
2. bone haft

the Dry Run bridge and south of the Batavia Pike. It is composed entirely of flat limestones, of various sizes and thicknesses, and covered with about two feet of clayey loam. It is nine feet high and has a diameter, at base, from east to west, of sixty feet. It has been opened in its center to a depth of five feet; a layer of charcoal and ashes had been reached when the work was discontinued."(5) This mound still exists although in the last fifty years it has been further reduced by a second excavation. Shortly after the Turner Works were excavated, a number of local farmers dug into numerous tumuli in the Newtown area seeking more of the precious gold which had been found by Dr. Metz and his staff.

On the Hermitage Club's property North of Lawyer Road and just West of the East Fork of Jenny's Run is situated the George Hack Stone Mound (33-Ha.-40). The terrain is deeply eroded due to the long years of farming prior to the acquisition of the land by the Hermitage Club. Just northeast of the stone mound is a smaller earthen mound. Neither of the mounds exceeds two feet in heighth, their diameters both being twenty feet. A nearby historic cemetery should not be confused with either of these aboriginal mounds Surrounding the base of 33-Ha.-40 is a circle of standing stones similar to that within 33-Ha.-216. The stones of which this circle is constructed are much smaller than those at Sand Ridge, and appear to have been set on edge for the purpose of containing the mound. Forty years ago, this interesting containing wall was much more nearly intact than now, and consequently the mound was higher.

ADDITIONAL MOUNDS AND VILLAGE SITES IN ANDERSON TOWNSHIP

Anderson Township, bordered by the Ohio River on the south, the Little Miami on the west and north, and Clermont County on the east, has the densest concentration of archaeological sites in the county. Within the forty square mile township maximum elevations increase in an easterly direction, reaching a point over nine hundred feet above sea level near Cherry Grove; the valley floor having a minimum elevation of four hundred and fifty feet above sea level. The highlands are drained by a series of creeks emptying either into the Ohio or the Little Miami Rivers. Five Mile Creek and Eight Mile Creek drain to the Ohio. Dry Run, Jenny's Run and Clough Creek all drain into the Little Miami. All of these have a considerable flow during certain parts of the year, but they are usually dry during the summer months.

In the northeastern corner of the Township there are four Woodland Village Sites associated with the Turner Works. The first of these (33-Ha.-77) is located on Mr. Spees' property on the level terrace northeast of the Turner Works. A deep ravine divides the site into two unequal areas. Three long Flint Ridge flake knives, flakes, cores, blanks, and corner-notched projectile points were found on this site by the present survey. In 1952, Father Garvey, of St. Xavier High School in Cincinnati, dug a pit on the part of the site covered by a rifle range. At a depth of three feet he found a Middle Woodland pottery vessel and evidence of fire.

---

(5)*Ibid.*, p. 300

East of the corner of Mt. Carmel and Round Bottom Roads is situated a second Hopewellian Village (33-Ha.-45). Although it is now partially covered by the Norfolk and Western Railroad, the dimensions of the site are two hundred yards by seventy yards, with the longer dimension paralleling the railroad. The survey collected from this site thirty-three flakes, ten broken Flint Ridge flake knives, one small crude point, nine chert cores, one large Flint Ridge core from which flake knives had been flaked, and a few grit-tempered plain potsherds. Some sort of curved earthwork may once have existed at this spot, for it is sketched in by Dr. Metz in one of his unpublished manuscripts in the Peabody Museum.

One-half mile S.E. on Mt. Carmel Road, we find the third small village site. This one hundred yard by thirty yard site conforms to the gentle contours of a low terrace east of the road. In addition to material much like 33-Ha.-45, one polished celt and one grit tempered, cordmarked sherd were found. One hundred and fifty yards southwest from the last site stood the Broadwell Mound, named for an old family in the valley. This elliptical structure was seven feet tall and eighty feet on its long axis; it was removed in the 1920's.

The large field immediately west of the Cemetery Mound (33-Ha.-52) is the site of a large Hopewell village (33-Ha.-55), which we have called the "Denneman Site". The proximity of this site to the Turner Works as well as the artifacts recovered from it suggest that it is another one of the dwelling places of the people who constructed the cyclopean ceremonial center nearby. In addition, however, the presence of Archaic material at the Denneman site is attested to by the bevelled point mentioned below. The artifacts collected by the survey from this site include:

    1 Woodland leaf blade
    2 stemmed points (one bevelled)
    1 corner notched serrated point
    1 leaf shaped flake blade
    2 small stemmed points
    3 long chert side-notched blades
    2 Harrison County side or corner notched blades
    6 polished celts
    numerous flakes, cores, etc.

Mr. Denneman, the former owner of the site, has collected from it for over forty years. His collection consists of the following:

    23 polished celts
    1 grooved axe
    2 split and polished stones
    2 hammerstones
    3 scrapers
    8 drills
    30 triangular points (10 Ft. Ancient)
    39 stemmed points
    18 Woodland blades
    25 corner notched points

36 side notched points
4 double based points

In addition, dozens of flake knives from this site are in various local collections.

A cemetery (33-Ha.-138) of undetermined extent is located on the extreme northwestern point of the terrace on which the Denneman site is located. In the 1930's, two burials were dislodged while a pipeline was laid between the large hip-roofed barn and the smaller shed behind it. Placed with the burials were long, finely wrought ceremonial blades and mica, all of which are now in the collection of the Cincinnati Art Museum.[1]

Centuries after the upper terrace declined as a Hopewell town, the lower terrace was settled by the Ft. Ancient people. Many years ago a half dozen burials in the northern corner of the first terrace were laid bare by a spring flood. Beneath the skull of each skeleton had been placed a small, shell-tempered, cordmarked cup. One of these was recently donated to the Museum of Natural History by Mr. Robert Denneman. The vessel is very plain with no flare to the undecorated rim.

The field to the east of this cemetery is a Ft. Ancient village site, probably related to the above mentioned burials. The occupation level is at least two feet below the present surface, and the field was in grass at the time of the survey's first visit. When the field was newly plowed in the spring of 1956, two Madisonville plain sherds were found. Mussel shells, cores, flakes, firecracked rock and one scraper were also found at that time.

To the south of the above village site, there was, until 1957, a long elevated ridge on which Dr. Metz had located two mounds and a cemetery, as well as the Adena circle (33-Ha.-44) mentioned earlier. The northern point of the ridge was occupied by the cemetery (33-Ha.-211). In the late 1800's, numerous burials were found here, but data as to their positions and associated artifacts was not recorded. Although isolated artifacts are usually of little scientific value, a unique gorget found at the foot of the terrace below the cemetery may shed some light on aspects of early trade. The artifact appears to be made of fossilized bone. The nearest source for that material is at Big Bone Lick, twenty-eight miles distant in Boone County, Kentucky. One end of the highly polished utensil was tapered to an awl, while in the center of the tool are three holes similar in spacing to the bone gorgets found in the Newtown Focus. Photo pg.53.

Two hundred yards south of the preceding site were two mounds aligned east to west and three hundred feet apart (33-Ha.-212, 213). Dr. Metz designated them Group C, numbers 20 and 21. The height of 33-Ha.-213 was eight feet, the circumference was two hundred fifty feet. Both of these mounds were graded off in 1957; observers from the Cincinnati Museum of Natural History who watched the bulldozing reported that nothing of archaeological interest was found.

Across Round Bottom Road from the Edwards Stone Mound (33-Ha.-205) is a small knoll upon which artifacts have been found. As

---

[1]Mr. Aicholtz, who owns the barns near which the cemetery is located, supplied this information.

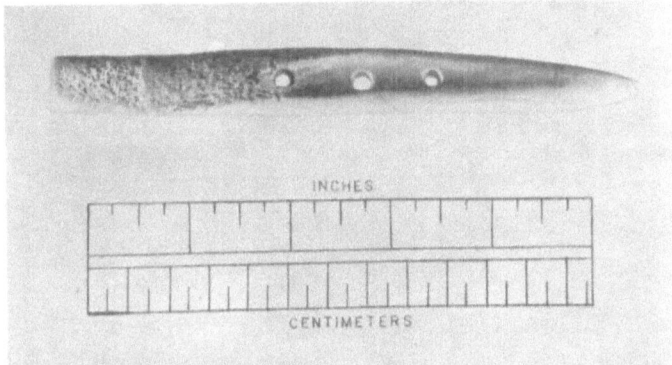

Mineralized bone gorget from Anderson Township. (33-Ha-221)

at many villages in that area, the small "bird points" are found in approximately equal numbers with the larger stemmed points. In addition to a half dozen of each of these two types, a simple unexpanded drill, blanks, flakes, and both corner and side notched points are reported from the knoll. Although areas of greater concentration of occupational evidence are detectable, broken points, hammerstones, and the usual village debris fairly cover the entire surface of the knoll.

The gravel pits opened on the other side of the valley involved the destruction of eight mounds. Unquestionably the most important mound of this group was the Martin Mound (33-Ha.-126). Dimensions given by Dr. Metz for the Martin or Walker Mound, as it is variously called, were as follows; circumference at base — six hundred and twenty-five feet, width at base — one hundred and fifty feet, diameter — two hundred and fifty feet, height — thirty-nine feet. The mound covered an area of an acre. For years, its owner protected the mound from erosion, but, much to Dr. Metz's consternation, refused permission to dig into the tumulus, preferring that the dead be allowed to "rest in peace." However, during the 1930's, an ingenious gentleman named Walker tunneled around in the bowels of the mound, strung up electric lights, and, by charging a nominal admission fee, made enough money to pull himself out of the Depression. The bulldozer operator whose job it was to level the mound, still recalls, two decades later, digging through many log tombs. From his accurate description, it is evident that the most common type of tomb was the simple two-dimensional log structure, constructed by laying two logs on each side of a rectangle around the body. Much material said to have been found in this major Adena mound is now in the Perry collection in Miamiville, Ohio, but an unusual tubular pipe inscribed with a bird-like pattern is the only artifact definitely ascribable to it.

The remaining mounds of this group are scattered over an area of one-half square mile. Three of them (33-Ha.-191, 2, 3) were arranged at two-hundred foot intervals in a line along Dry Run. The largest of the group was ten feet tall; the remaining tumuli were four feet high. In 1883, the Literary and Scientific Society of Madisonville excavated all three of them. Log tombs, the sure sign of the Adena Culture, protected all of

Martin or Walker Mound - Anderson Township

the twenty burials found in the largest of the three. Two other tumuli stood about a hundred yards west of the towering Martin mound. At least one of them was graded down for fill dirt prior to 1830, but, as so often happens, no data was kept which could tell us of its contents.

Limestone tempered plain pottery and Woodland artifacts are found in two of the hilltop village sites in the Newtown section of the valley. The first of these (33-Ha.-71) has been mentioned in Chapter Three. The second village is on the edge of the same range of hills, commanding a no less magnificent view of the valley. A slate hoe, polished celts, and stemmed Harrison County flint points have been found on 33-Ha.-72. Like the higher site, this one is in grass, making conditions for collecting very poor.

In and around the village of Newtown is a great concentration of valuable archaeological sites. The very existence of many of these sites would now be unknown had the early inhabitants of "Mercersberg" not taken an interest in archaeology.

In the Odd Fellows cemetery on Round Bottom Road near Newtown are situated two well-preserved mounds. The larger of the two (33-Ha.-20) is thirteen feet high and of an elliptical shape. To the northeast of that mound is 33-Ha.-21 which is completely covered with the graves of the earliest settlers of Mercersberg, or Newtown. It is not known whether any material of archaeological value was found when the graves were dug.

Immediately northwest of Newtown, on Turpin Farm property, is situated the Hahn's field site. This important Fort Ancient Aspect village, or more correctly, town covers an area one-quarter mile in diameter. Village debris is found over the entire surface of the site:

pottery — shell tempered
   8 plain rims
   1 paddle marked body sherd
  10 cordmarked body sherds
  14 plain body sherds
103 small triangular points
31 "turtlebacks" scraper or points
3 small thin cache blades
3 flake knives
3 Woodland blades
4 stemmed points
1 large stemmed base
5 side notched points
2 corner notched points
7 drills
2 hafted drills
1 bone punch
2 hafted scrapers
blanks, cores, etc.
2 shell disks
1 adze
1 granite sphere

    The Peabody Museum of Harvard University conducted a brief excavation here prior to 1900, and have in their collection many burials with which were found pottery vessels and other artifacts. At least two mounds once stood within the village, but none are detectable now or were noticeable within the last thirty years.[2] In the collections of the many local residents who frequent the site are copper beads, grooved axes, and discoidal stones. The grooved axes and numerous stemmed points are probably of Woodland origin, much like the stray artifacts which have been found at the Madisonville site. The Little Miami River once flowed past the west side of the village, making communication with the other Fort Ancient villages in the area easy (if they were contemporary), and providing a convenient source of food and water.

    Three-quarters of a mile to the northeast of Hahn's field and on the same terrace is located the Perin site. This previously unknown village site (33-Ha.-38) is one of the largest unstratified Woodland sites in the county. It conforms to the contours of the terrace north of the Perin nursery and west of the Newtown Road, covering an area of about four acres.

        pottery
          grit tempered
            23 cordmarked
            14 smooth

---

[2] Metz, Dr. Charles L., Unpublished letter to Prof. Putnam of Harvard. June 2, 1885. Peabody Museum, Cambridge, Massachusetts.

1 smooth rim
2 cordmarked rims
limestone tempered
19 smooth
21 cordmarked
1 smooth rim
5 large, thin, broken blades
15 broken points
8 Woodland leaf blades
4 corner notched points
13 side-corner-notched points
1 small triangular point
3 small corner notched points
10 stemmed points
9 roughed-out blades
8 blanks
1 flake knife
2 hafted scrapers
1 side scraper
5 drills
3 double base points
1 cupstone
1 slate hoe
1 roughed-out celt
7 polished celts
1 large mortar
numerous cores, flakes, hammerstones

It is improbable that the Perin Site is a component of the late Anderson Township Newtown focus. The absence of limestone gorgets and the scarcity of the "shoulder" type pottery vessels suggest a slightly earlier, more Hopewell-like Newtown occupancy. The entire area is now devoted to a tree nursery. Over the next five years, most of the saplings which now cover the site will be removed, disturbing the archaeological material beneath the surface. The depth of this site is not known, but silt covers the entire area.

Two small mounds once stood further to the south on Newtown Road, or Church Street as it is called within Newtown. Nothing is known of the contents of the first of these (33-Ha.-198) which stood in front of the old Methodist Episcopal Church. North of the above mound and on the opposite side of the Norfolk and Western track stood a third mound which was destroyed at the time Dr. Metz was active in local archaeology. This mound, which was seven feet high, contained human bones and charcoal from a fire that had evidently burned on the mound itself.

In the center of the village stood two extremely important Fort Ancient mounds (33-Ha.-201, 33-Ha.-210) which contained a burial trait which can now be considered as distinctive of Fort Ancient mounds in the Newtown area. The first of these was located at the junction of Church Street and Batavia Pike. Since the mound was removed in road building prior to 1830, no information as to its size was recorded. More important, however, is the surviving report that five skeletons arranged in a circle, with their heads toward the center of the mound, were found when the mound was graded down.

About one hundred and fifty yards to the northwest of the preceding mound was the second mound. Of this mound, Mr. William Edwards, who, according to Metz, was "a most intelligent and reliable observer," said:

> "The hands in the Newtown District were working on the road, when it became necessary to remove a small mound in front of Mr. Dunseth's house, in Newtown, where they found five skeletons, and a pot, apparently formed of mussel shells and a kind of glutinous cement. It would probably have held a gallon, and was perfectly formed in shape. It was found in the center of the mound, and the skeletons lying regularly around it, with their heads toward it as a common center. Several other mounds have been removed where the skeletons have been placed in the same positions."[3]

It is obvious from Mr. Edwards' precise description, that this was a Fort Ancient Mound. His mention of "several other mounds" with a similar burial pattern is significant as an indication that the Turpin mound is not unique in that respect and that this trait occurs frequently within the geographical area of the Madisonville focus.

Behind the fish hatchery in Newtown is located one of the loveliest plateaus in the area. Two fine old homes, one of them built by a son of Philip Turpin, dominate the level hilltop and command a view of the lower bottom-land. On the northernmost point of the plateau is a low irregular mound (33-Ha.143) which was one of the few truncated mounds in Hamilton County. Dr. Metz was the only early writer to mention this peculiar mound. He claimed that graded ways extended to the top from both the northern and the southern sides of the ten foot high tumulus.[4] The present owners of the land once found a skull on the hillside below the mound, but have never found any artifacts on the table land. The accuracy of Dr. Metz's report can only be tested by excavation. It is possible that this mound is similar to one in Whitewater Township which will be mentioned later.

---

[3] *Ibid.*, p. 298.

[4] *Ibid.*, p. 298.

A quarter mile southwest of the truncated mound is located a large Fort. Ancient village site (33-Ha.-34) on which in the past have been found more than two hundred burials. The burials found in the summer of 1838 were described by a Mr. T.C. Day:

> "Last summer, the workmen, in procuring gravel for the Batavia turnpike, immediately in the rear of Newtown, in the bank of a small stream called Jenny's Run, disinterred an immense number of human skeletons. This ancient burial ground is on a gravely point that juts out from the bank into the run forming an acute bend. The graves are not, on an average, more than two feet in depth, though probably they were a great deal deeper, as the ridge has evidently washed to a considerable degree. As far as caved, the point is a solid body of coarse gravel, till within about two and one half feet of the surface, which is composed of sand and loam. The skeletons lay in the sandy stratum between the gravel and earth, and so far as preservation is concerned, it has answered the purpose well. Whole anatomies have been exhumed in an excellent state of soundness, the teeth particularly, some of them as white as ivory, and perfect in every respect. Forest trees, such as beech, sugar maple and oak, some at least two feet in diameter, were growing immediately over the graves, and their gnarled roots twisted fantastically through the skulls of these remnants of ancient people. A fall of gravel would frequently bare the whole front of a grinning skeleton, seemingly thrust in the grave, feet foremost, and in fact the whole of the bodies bore evidence of a promiscuous burial, some placed horizontally, facing the west, others level, anon a group of four heads within a space of two feet, and in every imaginable position. About twenty feet from the first discovery of the bones, the workmen came to a large body of charcoal, and the remains of of a stone fireplace. An earthen vessel was found by some boys, which was broken and destroyed before an actual description could be obtained."[5]

From the above description it seems probable that some of the burials had been in storage pits. Very little remains of the gravely point, but the actual village site extends for eighty yards north to the Blum's home. Both this survey's collection and the Blum Collection show a predominance of triangular and side notched points, many hafted scrapers, and both plain and cordmarked shell tempered pottery. By far the most important and artistically the most valuable artifact from the village is a limestone pipe in the form of a human head, now in the Peabody Museum's collection. The features are cut into the soft stone in such a way that the head faces away from the smoker. Around the forehead is a narrow

---

[5] Day, T.C., *The Antiquities of the Miami Valley*, in "Cincinnati Chronicle," Nov., 1839.

band which delineates the forehead from the top of the bowl. Beneath this elevated band on both sides of the head where the ears should be are two flap-like projections. Although it cannot be definitely determined whether these were intended to represent hair, a head-dress or highly formalized ears, I am inclined to favor the latter. The same things occur rarely in carvings from the lower Mississippi valley and, strangely enough, in contemporary Anatolia, where the artists insist that the resemblance to ears is obvious.

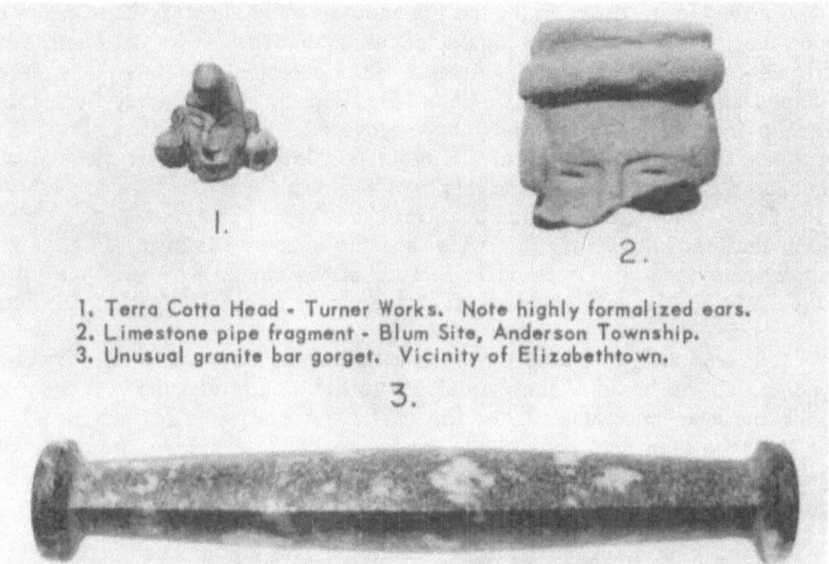

1. Terra Cotta Head - Turner Works. Note highly formalized ears.
2. Limestone pipe fragment - Blum Site, Anderson Township.
3. Unusual granite bar gorget. Vicinity of Elizabethtown.

Clogston and Metz Collections - Peabody Museum, Cambridge

In the early springtime, a nearly obliterated mound can still be detected in the Blum's field, not more than sixty yards from the site discussed above.

At the first broad terrace of the Jenny Run valley is the former home of Col. William Jewett, near which stood the nine foot high Jewett Mound (33-Ha.-32). The course of Newtown Road was changed in 1952 and the mound was bulldozed at that time. The undisturbed floor should be carefully excavated in order that any postmolds or other features may be uncovered. Nearby, on the terrace next to the Jewett home stands a projection resembling a mound, nearly four feet high, covered with large trees (33-Ha.-33).

On the high hilltop between the Jewett mound and Clough Creek stands a mound which is now barely visible, but was once "nearly eight feet tall."[6] (33-Ha.-233). For some completely unfathomable reason, local residents refer to it as the "Snake eaters' mound." Since they prefer not to let strangers into their Mysteries, the reason for the epithet will remain unknown. Another group of three tumuli, known as the Bullock Mounds, was excavated by Dr. Metz in 1889. These were situated on the high ridge of land between Jenny's Run and Clough Creek.

---

[6] *Op. cit.*, Metz, pp. 303 and 881.

The first of these, Mound A, was three feet high and elliptical, with a length of sixty feet and width of forty. It contained village debris such as potsherds and flint, but the only distinctly recognizeable artifacts recovered were three "flints" and a slate ornament. The ornament is thin and circular, with one side slightly squared off and drilled. Mound B was two hundred feet north of Mound A, had a diameter of forty feet, and was two and one-half feet high. There can be little doubt that this mound contained a simple log tomb. Dr. Metz reported that long timbers were arranged in a rectangle, the dimensions of which were four and one half feet by six feet. Once again, occasional loads in the fill contained fragments of charcoal and pottery. Two ceremonial points, one drop shaped and five and one-half inches long, and the other stemmed and four inches long were the only artifacts recovered. Mound C, the last of the Bullock Group, was elliptical and eight feet high. The short dimension, measured east to west, was eighty feet while the length measured eighty-five feet. Two skeletons had been interred there. The first was in a log tomb ten feet long by six feet wide, and the second was simply placed on a prepared surface. A peculiar feature of the mound was an "ash pit" three feet by eleven feet by two feet deep, which contained one lone celt.

It seems safe to classify the Bullock Mounds as a group built by one people, on the basis of their proximity to each other and the presence of such common cultural traits as log tombs. A more detailed examination of the area than was possible in the course of this survey would be of great value since it might locate the village site from which the loads of charcoal, pottery, and refuse were taken.

At the back of the same range of hills on which the "Snake Eaters' Mound" and the George Hack Stone Mound are situated, and near the corner of Lawyer Road and Little Dry Run Road, is the Lawyer village site (33-Ha.-47). In Dr. Metz's time this early Woodland village was traceable by a deep overburden of midden; erosion has now reduced it to a thickness of nine and a half inches. Since the site was being destroyed at the time of the survey, a brief excavation was conducted which, although unproductive of post molds, burials, etc., did recover the following:

5 crude celts
4 polished celts
1 chisel
1 hammerstone
4 scrapers
1 Silurian coral
3 limestone tempered plain sherds
1 linestone tempered cordmarked sherd
2 quartz tempered cordmarked sherds
3 broken projectile points
2 "fishtail" points
5 Woodland blades
1 slide notched projectile point
1 stemmed projectile point

The pottery appears to be the typical Early Woodland type. The "fishtail" points are also found at other Early Woodland sites in the county. More unusual are the two five-inch long blades and the bowl made from a human skull which were found by friends of Dr. Metz. The hill above the Lawyer site was once crowned with a three foot high mound which stood just off Little Dry Run Road (33-Ha.-215). Its location is reminiscent of the Adena hilltop mounds; its proximity to the Lawyer site may indicate a connection between the two.

The Clough Creek Valley, and the hills which flank it, has surprisingly few detectable archaeological sites in it. This may be due in part to the annual flooding which leaves a thin deposit of silt in the valley and the ruinous erosion of the hills. But the majority of the sites are crowded around the mouth of the creek.

The only significant site in the valley is a six foot high mound which once stood on the arm of land jutting into the valley east of the junction of Corbly and Clough Roads (33-Ha.-220).

One half mile north of the mouth of the creek, on the terrace surrounding the old Philip Turpin home, is an extremely important concentration of late Woodland-Fort Ancient material.

The terrace is approximately one-eighth of a mile long and one hundred yards wide, with the longer dimension following the base of a large hill. Its height of ten feet above the plain renders it safe from floods and the swampy conditions which prevail in the bottoms during the winter months. Water was readily available, since the Little Miami River once flowed past the base of the terrace, where McCollough's Run now barely trickles.

In spite of the scientific excavations of the Turpin Farm, by the Peabody Museum and by the Cincinnati Museum of Natural History (1946-49); and the annual pilgrimages performed by the faithful of the collecting world, the site has large areas which are completely unexplored.

The earliest known inhabitants of the Turpin site were the Newtown focus Woodland people. Their presence is known by the stone mound, and the Woodland village, which underlies the later Fort Ancient village (33-Ha.-19). Square huts dotted the Turpin site during the "Newtown" period. Very briefly, the ceramics of the Newtown focus are distinguished by the following: crushed rock tempering; predominantly cordmarked surfaces; unmodified or flattened rims; usually angular (more rarely rounded) "shoulder"; round perforations below the lip or, rarely, rectilinear decorations. See picture on next page.

Toward the close of the Woodland period, the Fort Ancient people moved in. Like the "Newtown" folk, they built square houses, but their shell tempered jugs were a new southern innovation. Whether there was any intergroup contact is as yet not definitely known, but both the Woodland material and the Fort Ancient material strongly suggest such intercourse.

In the Fort Ancient period, we find another of the mounds with the circular "wagon wheel" burial pattern. Unlike the small mounds mentioned earlier, this one (33-Ha.-159) stood over six feet high and contained one hundred and sixty burials, one hundred of which were part of

"Newtown focus" house site from the Turpin village.

Profile in the Turpin village showing the line delineating the Newtown or "Old Village" stratum from the more recent Ft. Ancient level.

Turpin Mound before Excavation – Anderson Township

the spoke pattern. A further parallel between this mound and those like it in Newtown is the unusually low percentage of burials with artifacts in association. Four occurred at 33-Ha.--159, whereas no artifacts at all are mentioned in direct association with either of the Newtown mounds.

Two carved bone objects from the Fort Ancient village are of great interest. The first is a fragment of bone upon which two snakes have been carved in low relief. It is obvious from the shape of the heads and the decorations on their backs that one is a rattlesnake and the other is a copperhead. The rattlesnake's appearance is all the more surprising since it is not, or has not recently been, indigenous to southwestern Ohio. The second object is the standing figure of a man carved in low relief on the end of a hairpin. In its left hand is a cross-hatched object that suggests a fish. His body is naked except for what appears to be a loin cloth. Around the forehead is a band surprisingly like the one on the pipe from the nearby Blum site. Also, on the sides of the head near the ears are raised and delineated forms which could be either the hair or some sort of head dressing.

A stone pipe in the shape of a human figure which was found on the surface of the site sheds further light on the hair and hat styles of the Fort Ancient people. It clearly shows a circular hat which was worn over hair pulled into a single braid in back.

Sixty yards to the west of the old farm house is a third mound which is now barely visible. Its present height is about one foot but, at the present rate of erosion, it will be completely obliterated within the next few years. Its surface is covered with Ft. Ancient village debris. Whether the debris was dragged there by the plow, or deposited on the mound in prehistoric times cannot at present be determined.

On the prominent hill directly to the south of the Turpin site there were, until 1934, a low mound and a cemetery (33-Ha.-161, 162). Signal Hill, as it is now called, is built over with comfortable homes so it is impossible to find from direct evidence if the "cemetery" was actually a village site. However, Dr. Metz mentions extended burials beneath flat slabs of limestone in this locality (7) — a typical Fort Ancient burial technique. Kopf and Kopf, Inc., builders of the Signal Hill subdivision, encountered four extended burials with which had been placed pottery vessels, over fifty projectile points, of various types, and the bones of a small animal. The doglike bones were found near the skull of one of the skeletons. A circle of red clay enclosed the burials and fresh water mussel shells were scattered throughout the nearby dirt. More recently, local residents have reported the findings of projectile points and occasional sherds. It is very likely that this was actually a small Fort Ancient village, although it is quite surprising to find evidence of a Fort Ancient community on such elevated terrain.

A second elevated, isolated Fort Ancient village is on the five hundred and ten foot high range of hills to the southwest. The Sand Ridge site (33-Ha.-16) is in many respects unusual and different from the other Madisonville Focus sites further up the valley. Conover's excavations indicated a stratification of Newtown focus - Fort Ancient material. His observation is borne out by the Museum's as well as Philip Nunn's collection of pottery:

---

[7]*Ibid*, Metz, p. 302.

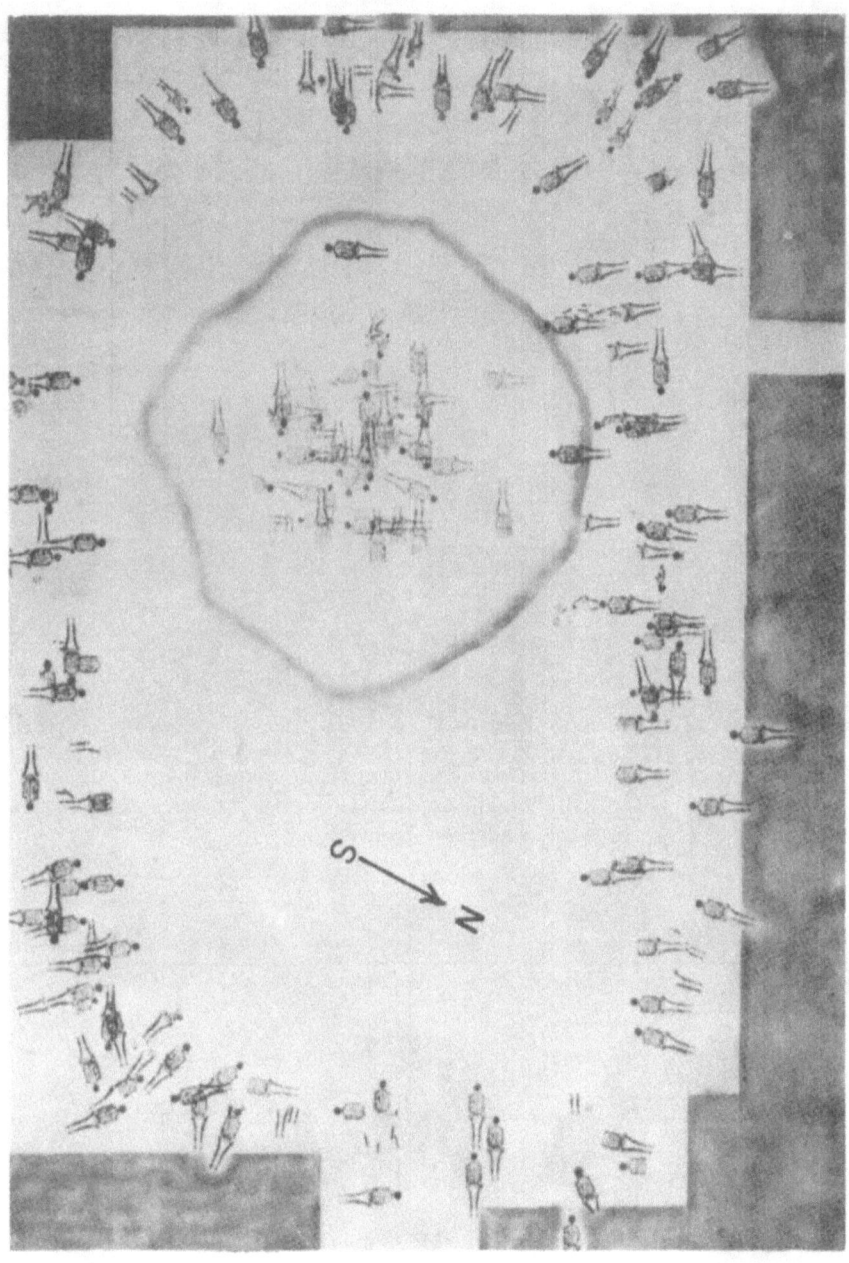

"Wagon Wheel"-like burial pattern surrounding the principal Turpin mound. Dark line denotes area covered by tumulus.

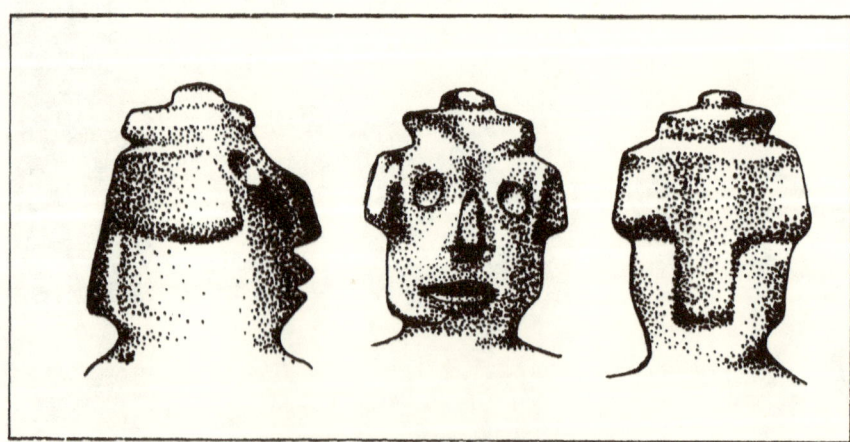

Snake Effigies and Bone Hair Pin, Turpin Site
Anderson Township

Head of Effigy Pipe, Turpin Site
Anderson Township

Pottery:
  Grit tempered:
    4 cordmarked, very heavy grit
    21 cordmarked, medium grit
    5 plain, medium grit
    1 squared rim (vertically cordmarked)
    1 round handle
  Limestone tempered:
    9 cordmarked
  Shell tempered:
    59 cordmarked
    4 plain
    9 plain rims
    6 "very unusual" sherds and decorated rims

The "very unusual" sherds are of Newtown Focus and Fort Ancient manufacture. The first is a big handle decoration in the form of a turtle-like animal. A still more unusual piece is the strange bird-like form which hovered above the rim of a pot, looking in toward the center. This large figure is unique in Fort Ancient art. The last two Fort Ancient sherds are rims, one decorated with large punctuations, and the other a fragment of what must have been either a scalloped lip or merely a pouring spout. The punctuated sherd has hatching on the inside of the flared and expanded lip.

The Newtown people at Sand Ridge produced equally strange pottery. One specimen is a squared rim which has deeply punched holes in a row around the inside. Each hole is about one eighth inch in diameter and was obviously punched while the clay was still in the plastic state. Another squared rim has punched decorations on the flat top of the lip. On the inside of the same sherd is a linear decoration which, by the addition of only a few more strokes, would be a guilloche pattern. The last Newtown sherd is fabric impressed and has a rectilinear pattern around the rim.

These fragments of pottery, together with the peculiar location of the site and its proximity to others in the valley, make Sand Ridge by far the most challenging of the late prehistoric villages in Anderson Township.

In light of the importance of Sand Ridge, it is very satisfying to know that the present owners are preserving it from the weather and from thoughtless collectors as best they can.

Between the Sand Ridge site and Clough Creek is a terrace similar to the one at the Turpin farm on which is situated a large, stratified site covering an area of one thousand seven hundred square yards. The Clough Creek Site (33-Ha.-16) has not as yet been excavated, but it is likely that it, like the Turpin and Sand Ridge sites, extends to a depth of nearly five feet. Over a period of two years the survey has accumulated a representative collection:

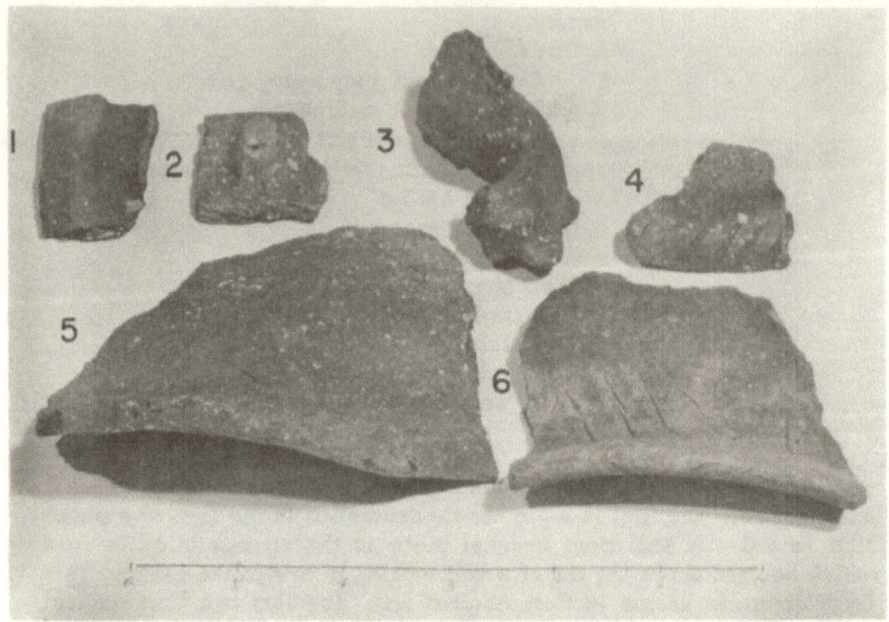

Ft. Ancient Pottery from Sand Ridge, Anderson Township
1. Punctuated Rim
2. Turtle (?) head on lug handle
3. Bird (?) mounted above flaring lip.
4. Incised pattern on inside of rim
5. Scalloped lip
6. Rectilinear decoration on Rim.

"Newtown" Pottery from Sand Ridge, Anderson Township
1. Punctuated rim (inside)
2. Linear Pattern on inside of punctuated lip
3. Fabric impressed ware with linear decoration
4. Simple squared and cordmarked rim sherd.

11 cores
14 blanks
1 chert chopper
numerous flakes of chert, and Flint Ridge flint
12 crude chert points
27 scrapers and flakes with secondary flaking
7 hammerstones
10 pecked and polished celts 4"-8", light to heavy; slate to granite
1 roughed out celt
1 broken pole shaped celt
2 broken limestone rectangular gorgets
1 broken polished banded slate object
1 banded slate chapper
1 slate hoe
1 chopper (similar to European hand-axe)
4 small well-worked corner notched points
1 thin side notched points
6 small stemmed points
6 large stemmed points
29 Ft. Ancient points
32 chert Woodland tear-shaped points
Pottery
   shell tempered
      457 smooth
      46 smoothed cordmarks
      7 cordmarked
      17 rims
      2 handles
      5 decorated
   grit tempered
      23 smooth
      2 cordmarked
      4 smoothed cordmarks
      3 squared rims
   limestone tempered
      109 smooth
      109 cordmarked
      2 rims

The very high percentage of smooth shell tempered ware is in sharp contrast to the Sand Ridge Site which is only one hundred and fifty yards away. Likewise, we find none of the Sand Ridge type of exotic, unusually-shaped vessels in the Clough Creek village. It is inconceivable that the Sand Ridge Fort Ancient people were contemporary to the Madisonville focus community dwelling on the terrace below them. One group, therefore, had to precede the other. In order to answer the question of temporal precedence, we will have to take into account other factors; they will be dealt with in connection with the village which produced them.

On the hills along Beechmont once stood two prominent mounds which have now been either partially or totally obliterated by time. The first of these (33-Ha.-218) was eight feet high and crowned a bluff east of Beechmont Avenue near Mt. Washington. The site of the second (33-Ha.-219) which was twelve feet high, is now covered by modern suburbia; there is no information extant concerning the contents or precise dimensions of either of these tumuli.

On the southwest corner of Birney Lane and Beechmont Avenue was a small, three and one half foot high mound which has now been destroyed (33-Ha.-180). An old resident of the area recalls it as being very low, and only discernible when the field was bare.

On the lands of E. Grischy, to the north of Salem Pike is a village which has produced a great quantity of non-ceramic artifacts. Springs occur over the whole level area along Putnam Road, and probably account for the great quantity of prehistoric artifacts which have been found there. Three-eighths of a mile north-northwest of the Grischy site is a mound of undetermined size. It commands a fine view of the Little Miami Valley due to its location on a peninsula of the land jutting out from the main body of the hill. The dense growth of briars and poison ivy rendered it impossible to measure the mound accurately, but it appears to be at least five feet in height.

The Cincinnati Water Works covers the site of a second Fort Ancient village which has produced some rather strange material. As was frequently the case, this community chose a dry, elevated terrace near a river for its village (33-Ha.-8). William C. Jewett, a civil engineer employed by the city, built the Water Works in about 1885 and during the construction, was able to rescue the collection upon which this discussion is based. The three-hundred and ninety-five sherds making up his collection can be broken down as follows:

```
177 Madisonville plain
235 Madisonville cordmarked
 19 no exterior surface
  7 salt pan sherds (crude with roughened exterior surface)
 16 grooved paddle marked
  1 non-Newtown focus grit tempered sherd
```

A "pottery pestle" similar to those from the Clover Complex in West Virginia was also recovered. Of the pottery, Edward V. McMichael of the University of Indiana observed:

> Handles are more like the ones from Turpin than Madisonville; decorations, while including the usual circulinear guilloche, include some odd motifs most like some from the Bintz Site in Kentucky.[8]

The Bintz site is only a few miles up the Ohio River from the Water Works village. It is not a matter for surprise that certain interaction

---

[8] McMichael, Edw. V.; *personal communications*; July, 1958

Ft. Ancient Pottery from Water Works Site - Anderson Township
(Indiana Historical Society)

existed between the two groups, but rather that such communities as those at Turpin, Clough Creek and Hahn's field were not also influenced by the Bintz focus.

Harrison County flint implements are found at a nearby site on the old Ebersole estate. The Ebersole Site (33-Ha.-3) was mentioned earlier as having produced a fluted point (#6); an ungrooved boatstone, and other polished artifacts, as well as stemmed points have also been found on this low-lying campsite.

On a terrace above the Coney Island Amusement Park, and below the Whetstone Stone Mound (33-Ha.-181) is a Woodland village site which is still quite prolific of artifacts. Grooved axes, celts, small and large notched points, Adena stemmed points and occasionally Fort Ancient material is found here. While laying a pipeline in the deep mantle of midden a number of years ago, the owner of the site found a burial. Unfortunately, he is unable to supply any data as to the position of the skeleton or the method of interment.

One half mile further out in the Ohio valley is the range of hills formerly known as "Hawkins Ridge." On the outermost brow of the seven-hundred and seventh foot hill is a group of five mounds aligned in a northwest-southeast row and touching one another.[9] The total length of the group is one hundred forty-five feet, the average width being about thirty-five feet. Those to the east are higher than the western tumuli, the heights ranging from six feet to three feet. In every case, the present heights are an unreliable indication of their original state, since collectors and curiosity hunters have dug large holes into all of them.

[9] *Op. cit.*, Metz; Dr. C.L.; *Prehistoric Monuments of Anderson Township*, p. 304.

There can be no doubt that this strange group of mounds (33-Ha.-182) is of aboriginal origin; first, because their location is typical of many hilltop tumuli — Mt. Lookout, Norwood, and many miles of the Ohio Valley are visible from them — and second, the people who "pothunted" them would probably not have climbed the hill to dig more than one hole had they not been encouraged or actually rewarded by their finds. A second example of a row of contiguous mounds will be discussed later. (See Miami Twp.)

Fifty yards northeast of this site is another mound (33-Ha.-183) which was, in 1881, six feet high and sixty feet in diameter but is now barely discernible. Its proximity to the other five suggests a possible relationship. The final mound in this group of seven was destroyed in the 1860's or 70's when the Hawkins home was built. Although it was on the same range of hills on the other six, it was two hundred yards north of 33-Ha.-183, from which point is is impossible to see the Ohio River Valley. When it was graded down, an extended burial covered with a layer of charcoal which "had been placed there after it had cooled",[10] was found on the floor of the mound. A triangular projectile point was found embedded in the cranium. It is unfortunate that more precise information concerning this mound has not come down to us.

On the down-stream side of the mouth of Five Mile Creek is another camp or small village (33-Ha.-6) which yields a surprisingly high percentage of Harrison County (Indiana) flint. In addition to the flakes there is one side-notched point and two scrapers of the same material, both carefully worked, and a chert scraper. Erosion is progressing to rapidly in the area that the village will be destroyed before long. An elevation suggesting a mound is on the opposite side of the creek.

Five Mile Creek forms a small, secluded valley through the hills which lies about a quarter mile from its mouth. In that valley, on the lower lands of Norman Rehg is a habitation site. Three pestles, three grooved axes, and three celts are in the Rehg collection. At the time the survey visited the site, the field was in grass, but one celt, a side-notched point, and numerous flakes and cores were found. The occurrence of pestles, grooved axes and celts at the same small site is, to say the least, unusual and perhaps not beyond suspicion.

Beyond the end of Thornhurst Lane on Watch Hill is a Woodland village site (33-Ha.-50). To date, it has yielded only projectile points but an examination of the surface produced sufficient burnt and fire-cracked rock, shell and flint flakes and cores to remove all doubt of its being a more or less permanent settlement. Woodland drop-shaped blades and stemmed points predominate, but side-notched and Fort Ancient and Woodland triangular points have been found. Beyond a spring to the southwest was once a small earth mound (33-Ha.-185) which, judging from its proximity, may have been built by the same people who occupied the village. Its location on an elevated tongue of land enabled it to command a broad view of the Ohio valley below. Prior to the time when Watch Point Drive was built, the mound stood fully eight feet tall and was conical in shape.[11]

---

[10] *Op. cit.*, Metz, Dr. C. L.; *Prehistoric Monuments of Anderson Township*, p. 303.
[11] *Ibid.*, p. 304

Two hundred yards northwest from Markley Road, before its intersection with Bennett Road, is an early Woodland village site. Even after over one hundred years of continuous plowing the area of the site can be readily discerned by the circular, five thousand square yard crown of rich midden on the knoll. The topography of the area and the cultural material from this site bear a strong resemblance to the Lawyer site. (And. Twp.) Both are in rolling country broken by high hills, and both are built on knolls. The two limestone tempered, cordmarked sherds from the Markley site are similar to the limestone tempered sherds from the Lawyer village. The great number of celts from both sites are similar, as are the Woodland blades and stemmed points. An important difference is the occurrence of corner-notched points at (33-Ha.-78). Unfortunately, the collections from both sites are so small that more detailed comparison is impossible.

There is a small campsite of undetermined extent on the hill on the opposite side of Markley Road, above its junction with Five Mile Road. The inaccessibility of the hilltop precludes the existence of a large community (33-Ha.-96); Dr. Metz collected here and the paucity of material, even in his day, bears out that conclusion.

Dropping back to the Ohio Valley, we come to an interesting site at the mouth of Eight Mile Creek (33-Ha.-5). Its entire area is strewn with village debris. In the center of the site is a moundlike projection approximately four feet high. Mr. Zeter, who has farmed the land for years, observed that on that one spot must have been an Indian tool maker's shop because he had found "over a bushel" of arrow heads and axes while plowing there. In shape, the "mound" is comparable to the one at the mouth of Five Mile Creek. If it is natural, which seems likely, it is nevertheless the center of the village; if it is the work of man, it must be determined whether it was built up by the deposit of midden or whether it was intentionally thrown up for funerary purposes. We must wait for an excavation to learn the answer.

The artifacts from the village appear to be of Newtown focus origin. Nearly half of the pottery is limestone tempered and cordmarked, the remainder is, in order of frequency, grit and limestone tempered, cordmarked; limestone tempered, smooth; and grit and limestone tempered, smooth.

Broken celts (polished and unpolished), stemmed projectile points, drills, hammerstones, a mortar and a piece of unworked cannel coal complete the collection. The relatively small area of this site and the homogeneity of the material found on it, would make it an excellent source for the study of the Newtown focus.

The final site in Anderson Township is one half mile further east in the Ohio valley, straddling the county line. The Eight and One-Half Mile site (33-Ha.-68) is oblong in shape, following the brow of the second terrace for a third of a mile. The following artifacts were found by the survey:

        3 loaf shaped pestles
        1 large mortar

Decorated Vessel from Haffner-Kuntz Site
Columbia Township

    1 bi-pitted cupstone
    3 unpolished celts
    9 polished celts
    1 ¾ grooved axe
    8 hammerstones
    6 blanks
    4 scrapers
    9 stemmed points
    4 side-notched points
    4 corner-notched points
    6 large, crude blades
    6 unstemmed points
    2 drop blades
    8 broken points
Pottery
    1 grit tempered plain
    1 grit tempered cordmarked
    4 limestone tempered, cordmarked
    1 limestone tempered, squared rim

Cultural material is sparsely distributed over the whole area, with the exception of the pottery, which is found most frequently in the center of the site. The wide range of artifact types make the task of dating the community (or communities) difficult, but it can be safely said that both Archaic and Early Woodland peoples inhabited this spot.

ADDITIONAL MOUNDS AND VILLAGE SITES IN COLUMBIA TOWNSHIP

Sharing the Little Miami valley with Anderson Township is Columbia Township. Although bordered by both the Ohio and the Little Miami, it does not contain the great concentration of archaeological wealth which we found in Anderson Township. This is due to two reasons; first, the greater part of its area is devoid of large streams and good water supplies, and second, the modern community has expanded so fast over most of the township that little note was made of any prehistoric monuments in the way. Nevertheless, twenty-eight sites are worthy of note here.

The first of these (33-Ha.-9) was located on a river terrace just northeast of the Kellogg Avenue bridge. Until 1957, this large Fort Ancient site was hidden beneath three feet of silt. At that time, however, the owner, who is in the topsoil business, dug away two-thirds of its area, leaving an exposed wall upon which the occupation level was readily discernible by the layer of shells, charcoal, etc.

The power shovel operator who stripped the site said that, in places, the midden, primarily shells, had been three to four feet thick. Numerous burials, pottery vessels and other artifacts were loaded onto the dirt trucks. One of the pottery vessels was of the Middle Mississippi long-necked water bottle shape, a form which occurs but rarely this far east.

When the remaining portion of the site came to the attention of the survey, four five foot blocks were excavated. Within that small area were two extended burials, one in a limestone slab-lined tomb, the other

Cleaned profile at the Haffner-Kuntz site, Columbia Township. Note plowed zone and deep stratum of shell midden. Picture taken during the survey's 1958 excavation.

having a pottery vessel with it, evidence of fire, sporadic post molds, and great quantities of potsherds. Over three-fifths of the sherds are Madisonville plain ware, the remainder being divided equally between cordmarked and smoothed-over cordmarks. Beneath the plowed zone and above the occupational level were occasional fragments of shell and/or grit tempered ware. They were so soft and weathered that the surface finish could not be determined. As at most Fort Ancient villages, refuse pits containing animal bones, charcoal and vegetable matter were found. Charcoal from one of these pits is being dated by the University of Michigan, and should produce results valuable to the understanding of Fort Ancient chronology.

Columbia Township was first settled in November, 1788,[1] by a group of twenty families from New York and New Jersey, led by Major Benjamin Stites. On the same elevated terrace which they chose for a cemetery there is also a "Newtown focus" village site (33-Ha.-15). The Columbia Baptist Cemetery is located between Lunken Airport and the Pennsylvania Railroad yards, which now cover part of the village. The only signs of habitation found on the site were mussel shells, flint flakes and cores, hammerstones and two limestone and grit tempered cordmarked sherds, but the entire terrace is covered with rich, black kitchen midden.

---

[1] Abbott, John S. C., *History of Ohio*, Tyler & Co., Detroit, 1875, p. 317.

Continuing out the Little Miami valley, we come to the Adena circle mentioned earlier (33-Ha.-168). Two hundred yards to the south of that earthwork was a mound (33-Ha.-169) which was removed for fill dirt in the early 1820's. Its dimensions are not recorded in the literature, but it is known that it contained a stone-lined tomb containing two extended burials, the faces of which were covered with layers of mica.

The five acres west of the above mound are described by Dr. Metz as a "cemetery."[2] He delineates the area by Elmwood, Walnut, Oak and Maplewood Avenues. All of these street names are those given by the Linwood Land Company in the 1870's and early '80's; although none of the present streets bear the same names, it is not difficult to relocate the general area. It is a broad terrace, typical of those chosen by Fort Ancient or Newtown people for their villages. It seems probable that the site is actually a village, not a cemetery, and that Dr. Metz's observation that "most of the heads are aligned toward the East"[3] is based more on coincidence than intention.

Another small but productive mound (33-Ha.-171) stood a few yards east of the Linwood station (now a storage shack) of the present Pennsylvania Railroad. Messrs. Hill, Hooker and Metz excavated the part of it which was not destroyed when the Little Miami Valley Railroad was built, but did not publish a report of their findings.

Miami Avenue leads from Eastern Avenue to the crest of a thirty-five foot high flat-topped hill. On the southernmost point of that hill is a Woodland village site (33-Ha.-35) which has produced thousands of flint and stone artifacts and small quantities of grit tempered, predominantly cordmarked pottery. Mr. Fluke of Terrace Park has most of the material in his excellent collection. The lithic artifacts include many grooved axes, pestles and corner-notched and stemmed points. Formerly, the land to the southwest of the village was the site of three mounds and a borrow pit; of two of the mounds we know nothing, the third was nine feet high in 1900, according to local residents. The borrow pit was three hundred yards distant from the mound and once surrounded by the remains of a wooden palisade.

On the hillside opposite 33-Ha.-36 and below Ault Park are five distinct terraces running for a considerable distance around the hill. Whether or not they are the works of Indians has for years been a source of controversy. From their location and general character, it seems highly improbable that they were constructed by men. As Fowke points out, they are completely ill-suited for occupation and[4] quite unnecessary, since there is an abundance of flat valley or table land nearby. There is a second example of terracing on Buffalo Ridge Road in Miami Township; the local explanation there being that they are buffalo trails. Another instance is at Fort Ancient where artifacts are found on the terraces a foot beneath the surface. Yet another occurrence is on the steep hillside of Hawkins Ridge in Anderson Township above the Coney

---

[2] *Op. cit.*, Metz, Dr. Charles L., 1878.

[3] *Op. cit.*, Metz, Dr. C.L., 1878, p. 5, 6.

[4] *Op. cit.*, Fowke, Gerard, p. 282.

Island amusement park. One must be cautious about ascribing their origin to Indians or to buffalo until the geological aspects have been carefully examined for the physical conditions under which slippage occurs are present in all four cases.

At the highest point in what is now Ault Park was a mound with an elevation of four feet.[5] Over the years its height was gradually diminished by erosion, and when the park was built it was completely obliterated (33-Ha.-172).

About a quarter mile to the southwest of Ault Park stood a second hilltop mound (33-Ha.-173). The old Anderson home, which has recently been torn down, covered the spot on which the mound once stood. No record was made by the Andersons of the contents or dimensions of the mound.

The final mound in this group was destroyed about 1910 when the area was developed. It was a quarter mile to the southwest of the preceding mound on the top of modern Mt. Lookout. A small mound, its height was four feet and diameter forty-eight feet.[6]

Duck Creek forms the best valley entrance to the interior of Columbia Township. One half mile up the valley from Red Bank Road and near the western end of the Pennsylvania Railroad bridge was a large mound (33-Ha.-175) above the Creek. Part of the mound is still visible, but most of its eight foot height and sixty-five foot diameter has been destroyed by recent building. Flakes of flint, firecracked rock and the usual village debris are found on the level, raised terrace next to the mound. A five foot high mound was located on the old Duncan estate in Hyde Park, one half mile northwest of the Duck Creek Mound. The Literary and Scientific Society of Madisonville briefly explored it and found only ashes and bones in the center of the floor. The site is now covered by new homes.[7]

Scattered over the broad terrace at Mariemont were formerly three distinct village sites and ten mounds in addition to the two circular earthworks and the fortification mentioned earlier. By far the most important historically is the Madisonville village site (33-Ha.-36), located on the westernmost extension of the ridge above "Whiskey Hollow." Beginning in the eighteen-seventies, organized excavations were conducted there for nearly half a century, but as many local collectors, curiosity seekers and gardeners know, the supply of burials, artifacts, and rich black soil is far from exhausted. It is not necessary to enumerate the finds at Madisonville, since so many excellent publications have described the site in great detail.[8] One unusual group of crystals

---

[5] *Op. cit.*, Metz, Dr. C. L., 1878, p. 6.

[6] *Ibid.*, p. 6.

[7] Metz, Dr. Charles L., Unpublished notes in the Peabody Museum, Cambridge. Massachusetts.

[8] See especially: Hooten, Ernest A., *Indian Village Site and Cemetery near Madisonville, Ohio,* Papers of the Peabody Museum of American Archaeology and Ethnology, Harvard University, Vol. VIII, No. 1, Cambridge, Massachusetts, 1920; and Griffin, J.B., *The Fort Ancient Aspect,* University of Michigan Press, Ann Arbor, 1943.

found by Mr. J.D. Conover suggests a far-flung trade of presently unknown extent. The six small crystals of staurolite were found deep within a refuse pit. Staurolite occurs in three major areas of the United States: New England, Minnesota and the Southeast. New England can safely be discarded as a possible source, although the mineral occurs abundantly in both Maine and New Hampshire, because nothing found at Middle Mississippi or Fort Ancient sites suggests such a contact. The Little Falls area of Minnesota seems improbable as a source for the same reason. However, staurolite not only occurs abundantly in the Georgia—North Carolina—Tennessee tri-state area, but the Madisonville focus exhibits many other artifact traits —especially pottery— which suggest direct southern contact. No other find in the Ohio—Indiana—Kentucky area of the Fort Ancient culture has suggested such distant trade contacts, making the staurolite find all the more important. Suspicion persists that they were "planted" at the site, which is not impossible, but if their occurrence there is not genuine, no evidence of "planting" was detected by the finder, who is a careful and thoroughly competent excavator.

Further insight into the chronology of Fort Ancient sites in the Little Miami Valley can be gained from the river's course. Aerial photographs show that, at one time, the river came within a few yards of the base of the terrace on the northwest. Likewise, the main stream once flowed by the Hahn's field site, seven-eighths of a mile away. If both sites were built when the river flowed by them, and if the river's meanders did not double back upon themselves, the two sites were not entirely contemporary, although their periods of occupancy might overlap.

In 1958, the Village of Mariemont built a swimming pool in the center of the site; during the clearing and grading, many burials, pits and artifacts were found. Near the pool, on the edge of the bluff above "Whiskey Run," there is still a deep, unexplored midden.

Two hundred yards north of the Madisonville site was a group of four mounds (33-Ha.-151), the largest of which was five and one-half feet in height. Dr. Metz's excavation of this mound revealed what appears to be a Woodland tumulus, probably associated with the nearby Woodland Village (33-Ha.-142).

The only reported excavation at that site, which is near the corner of Pleasant and Mariemont Avenues, was conducted by Mr. Robert Ward of Madisonville. He found two burials, stemmed points, and an expanded center limestone gorget. Material from the western edge of this site mingles with the eastern end of the Madisonville site, which led some early reporters to suggest that 33-Ha.-36 is stratified.[9] But when the swimming pool was being constructed at the Madisonville site, a number of excellent profiles of pipeline ditches were cleaned and examined by the author. There was nothing on any of them which would suggest a succession of cultures at the site.

The circular earthwork on the eastern end of the terrace mentioned above, was surrounded by a village and "four or five"[10] mounds. The

---

[9] In Griffin, 1943, are pictured a number of sherds which may have originated at the western extremity of this site.

[10] *Op. cit.*, Metz, Dr. C. L., 1878, p. 2.

sloping ground on which the village was located would ordinarily preclude a habitation site, but the slope is so gentle and the springs at the bottom so good, that its disadvantages were neutralized. Many Woodland artifacts from the Giauque collection are probably from this site (33-Ha.-147), but the documentation is such that we cannot be certain of that fact.

On the side of the earthwork near the center of Mariemont were four or five mounds with an average height of from three to four feet (33-Ha.-148). They were all obliterated by time before anything could be learned of their contents. A seven foot high mound near the center of the village met a similar fate (33-Ha.-149).

Leading from the Mariemont area to a point near Chillicothe was what Dr. Metz thought to be a clearly visible trail which had been used by the prehistoric men. In an effort to preserve the trail he undertook the tremendous task of placing rectangular stone markers, which were made for him and signed by a Madisonville tombstone cutter, at intervals along the entire route. His son, George, remembered clambering into the Metz family wagon on Saturdays with a marker — only one could be carried at a time on account of their weight — and planting it along the path which his father either saw or imagined. The approximate locations of two stones are known. The first is on the hillside south of the present route of Indian Hill Road as it winds up the hill from Madisonville in section 10; the second is in the area immediately north of the modern road before it turns to the southeast again to form the 10-11 section line. An old stone bridge still stands near the spot where the second marker is said to be.[11] Perhaps a thorough examination of Dr. Metz's papers, and a reexamination of the route would reveal what his intentions were and the basis for his conclusions.

One mile to the southwest of the Terrace Park Post Office, on the top of an eight hundred foot hill, was a group of seven mounds[12] which are no longer detectable. The floors and subfloors of these tumuli are probably still undisturbed (33-Ha.-204). At the base of the hill and across the Wooster Pike is a village site which covers an area seventy feet in diameter. Small quantities of both grit and shell-tempered pottery have been found there (33-Ha.-79). A large mound twenty-seven feet high once stood midway between the above site and Terrace Park (33-Ha.-203).

The Camden Mound, as it was called, was wrongly reported by Dr. Metz as having been destroyed when the Wooster Pike was constructed.[13] In his private notes, however, he corrects the error and gives a detailed account of his own excavation of the mound. It stood ten feet tall and was conical, the diameter being about eighty feet. A trench thirty feet wide was begun from the perimeter. After a brief search, two primary mounds, or small internal tumuli within the main structure, were found. The first was four and one-half feet high and twenty seven feet in diameter. Beneath the layer of fired stones, which extended from the

[11] This information was supplied by Mr. George Hack of Madisonville who was told it by the above mentioned son of Dr. Metz.

[12] Op. cit., Metz, 1878, shown on accompanying map only.

[13] Ibid., p. 9.

base to three quarters of the way up the side, was a three inch layer of clay. Eight skeletons were found in the first primary mound, all of them in the extended position. Upon the left-hand fingers of one skeleton had been placed five copper rings. With another were found a few copper beads.

The second primary mound was the same size and shape as the first and had the same peculiar crown of thin Clay. Near the center of the tumulus was found a two and one-half foot deep heap of pure gray ashes. This mound contained a total of twelve extended burials.

Looking again at the mound as a whole, we see that it is of a type which occurs frequently in southwestern Ohio. Two of the twenty individuals interred there were children, the remainder were adults. The only burial preparation seems to have been the layers of clay, one yellow and the other blue, which were placed beneath the skulls of two of the individuals. The artifacts were made of flint and copper; only one piece of unworked mica was found. Nothing can be said of the pottery other than that it did occur, because it has not been preserved in descriptions or in any of the known collections.[14]

The next two mounds are both located in the central part of the township; both are on the most prominent projections of high hills overlooking long valleys. The first one is the Benham mound in section 30 on the end of Grand Vista Avenue in Pleasant Ridge. Sometime prior to 1906, the mound was dug into to its floor by vandals.[15] "Mica, flesher, axes, chisels, and flint arrows"[16] have been found nearby or in the mound itself. In its present state of partial restoration, it is two feet lower than its original six foot height.

Near the water towers on Indian Mound Avenue is the Norwood Indian Mound. One of the finest and best preserved mounds in the county, it is thirteen and one-half feet high and elliptical in shape, its long axis being one hundred and thirty-one feet. Many of the mounds in the Mt. Lookout area and in Anderson Township were once visible from its top.

An isolated burial was found in Elmwood Place near the Procter and Gamble plant at about the end of the last century. With the skeleton had been placed a bone ornament and an unusual shell gorget. The bone ornament is a highly polished tube, two and seven-eighths inches long; around both ends are about two dozen small punctate decorations and in the center of the same side are two neatly drilled holes. The shell gorget is in the shape of a trapezoid, two inches long, and drilled in two places. Both are now in the Cincinnati Museum of Natural History collection. This burial is important in that it was found on very low land which was continually flooded by Mill Creek. Undoubtedly, there are many such sites in the Miami valleys also.

---

[14]Metz, Dr. Charles L., Unpublished notes and records. Peabody Museum, Cambridge, Massachusetts.

[15]Mr. Robert M. Booth supplied this information. His father built the house next to the mound in 1906.

[16]*History of Hamilton County*, 1881.

Norwood Mound — 33-Ha.-1

ADDITIONAL MOUNDS AND VILLAGE SITES IN SYMMES TOWNSHIP

Symmes township in the northeast corner of the county has been ignored as much by archaeologists as it was by prehistoric Indians. Two groups of stone graves — one at Symmes Station, the other near Loveland — are the only tumuli known in the township. Of villages, there are none. Instead, one can see innumerable small campsites which were occupied either by small family groups or were only inhabited for the brief span of time necessary to flake a few implements and to break a pot or two.

There is no reason to believe that the pre-Columbian population of of Symmes Township was as small as it now appears to have been. Indeed, many elegant polished stone and slate objects in the older collections attest to the presence of quite early inhabitants. But for years only sporadic interest was shown in the prehistory of the area since it has such a rich historical past; the old Christian Waldschmidt home and adjacent community along with the large Civil War training camp at Camp Dennison have distracted interest and attention from the more remote past. The gravel companies have made the situation still darker by removing many likely sites from the landscape in the days before their potential archaeological value was recognized.

Many of the floodland areas are slated to be developed in the next few years. In view of the profusion of sites only a few miles down stream, it would be quite surprising if no valuable discoveries are made at that time.

ADDITIONAL MOUNDS AND VILLAGE SITES IN SYCAMORE TOWNSHIP

Although the western border of Sycamore Township either contains the Millcreek Valley entirely or is formed by it, the high uneroded tableland further to the east typifies the greatest area of the township's topography. The creeks on the hills flow westward to Millcreek and are quite small until they reach the broad valley below. As one might expect, the majority of prehistoric remains are in the Millcreek valley or on the hills closest to it, the only major exception being the Adena circle mentioned above.

A small mound still stands in Sharon Woods where it is carefully protected by the Park Rangers (33-Ha.-236). Another once stood a short distance to the east of the town of Reading. A celt and a water-worn piece of cannel coal were taken from this mound before 1900. A third minor tumulus once stood in the Sharon Cemetery which is on the edge of a low terrace east of Sharonville.[1] (33-Ha.245) Southwest of the last mound and on the property of Dr. Forrest Beekley is a small village site (33-Ha.-102) which covers about half an acre on the small point to the south of Creek Road near Main Street. Dr. Beekley has found both stemmed and side-notched points, as well as two celts and a three-quarter grooved axe on the site.

Behind the Evendale School, which is on the corner of Reading and Glendale-Milford Roads, was a mound which has only recently been destroyed (33-Ha.-238). The only clue to the mound's cultural identity, and admittedly a questionable one, is the low knoll three-hundred yards to the north which is littered with flakes of Flint Ridge flint, cores and the usual debris found on prehistoric village sites. The top of the knoll, which must have been the center of the village, is now covered by a farmhouse; the western side is covered by Reading Road.

To the west of Millcreek are, in addition to the Crescentville earthworks, one mound and a campsite. The first (33-Ha.-122) is on the Matthew property on the hilltop to the north of Oak Road just before it descends into the valley. This mound stands in the Matthew dooryard and, in spite of its small size – only three feet in height – it is noteworthy as the supposed grave of an Indian named Opekasit. The legend persists and, until the recent change of ownership, many local residents bought milk from the Opekasit Dairy. The second, an unproductive campsite, (33-Ha.-125) is immediately south of Oak Road a few hundred yards west of the Opekasit Mound.

ADDITIONAL MOUNDS AND VILLAGE SITES IN SPRINGFIELD TOWNSHIP

To the west of Sycamore Township and north of Cincinnati is Springfield Township. Rolling hills extend across most of its six mile width, the West Fork of Millcreek and its tributaries being the only streams in

---

[1] *Op. cit.*, Olden, J. G , p. 18

the region. The West Fork valley should be carefully re-examined with probing equipment for the village sites in which the builders of the tumuli lived; the annual flooding of the creek has doubtlessly hidden many areas of habitation beneath tons of silt.

On the 685 foot hill which dominates the community of Lincoln Heights was a mound which, prior to its destruction in the 1920s, was six feet high and forty feet in diameter.[1] (33-Ha.-244) The few early Woodland artifacts known to be from the area suggest an Adena origin for the mound, but we cannot be certain that this is the case.

Section 10 contained two mounds, the contents of which were described in the 1870s. The first of these (33-Ha.-242) was situated "near Station spring on the Foster Farm",[2] which would be slightly north of the point at which Springfield Pike crosses West Fork. That this was actually an artificial tumulus is proven by Olden, who carefully and accurately described the load marks which he observed when the mound was being razed for the construction of the pike. The second was an oval mound (33-Ha.-243), the exact location of which is lost but which probably was near the Station Spring Mound. Its height was five feet and it stood two-hundred yards west of the excavation or 'borrow pit' from which the earth for its construction was taken. When it was dug into, a heap of ashes and charcoal were found, a trait reminiscent of certain Hopewellian mounds in Anderson Township.

Four hundred yards west of benchmark 659 on the property of Mr. Charles Burchenal is a picturesque mound seven feet high overlooking an isolated bend in the West Fork. No artifacts have been found either in the mound (33-Ha.-121), which was dug into at about 1850, or on the surrounding terrace, which is composed of clay and stone. See next page.

Southeast of the corner of Winton and Kemper Roads is a long knoll on which local collectors have found many celts, grooved axes and stemmed projectile points (33-Ha.-123). The half acre area in which artifacts are found is sharply delineated by the dark coloration of the soil resulting from village refuse. On Hamilton Pike near Houston Road is another site (33-Ha.-101) which has yielded many celts but no grooved axes, dozens of side-notched points but few stemmed ones. The people who have collected on these sites looked primarily for stone artifacts and made no record of any pottery which may have been there.

In the lowland near the new sewage plant on Compton Road is a habitation site which lies on the bank of the creek for a distance of over one hundred yards. (33-Ha.-124) Mr. Mulenhard of Woodlawn has over two hundred stemmed and corner notched points which are a part of a larger collection from this site.

In the north-central area of Springfield Township and in nearby Colerain Township are many so-called Indian mounds which are almost certainly no more than erosional relics of natural origin. The first two are both in Winton Woods, one near the lake and the other forming an island in it. Before the artificial lake was built, Dr. Glenn Black of Indiana and

---

[1] *ibid.*, p. 17
[2] *ibid.*, p. 18

Burchenal Mound — 33-Ha.-12 — Springfield Township

Mr. Ralph Dury of the Cincinnati Museum of Natural History visited these "mounds" and agreed that they were of natural origin. A more controversial "mound" is on the Pottenger farm on West Kemper Road in Colerain. It is elliptical and twenty-five feet in height, similar both in form and topographical location to the imposing formation near the Bintz site in Kentucky. The assertion of some local residents that skeletons have been taken from the Pottenger Mound, if there is any truth in it al all, is possibly based on the discovery of intrusive burials near its surface. The pigs who are penned at the base of the tumulus and who have assumed the monumental task of excavating it with their snouts have laid bare large stones near the top of the mound which are arranged suspiciously like the sedimentary slabs which one sees washing from the banks of a creek. Perhaps the pigs will continue their work and solve the problem for us.

ADDITIONAL MOUNDS AND VILLAGE SITES AT CINCINNATI

Looking across the broad plain at Cincinnati, the pioneer could see a confused maze of prehistoric earthworks and mounds in every degree of preservation. Many were barely discernible even in 1800 while others, like the Adena and Hopewellian earthworks mentioned earlier, were prominent landmarks of early Cincinnati.

The most famous of the mounds was the one in which the Cincinnati tablet was found (33-Ha.-224). From 1794, when "Mad Anthony" Wayne levelled off its top to construct an observation platform, until 1841 when it was completely removed, the mound suffered continual depredation. It stood near Fifth and Mound Streets and when first viewed by Europeans was thirty-five feet high and 147 yards around its elliptical base. Dr. Drake observed that the dirt for its construction had been taken from the thirty or forty yards immediately surrounding the mound.(1) This mound had many interesting constructional features which we can deduce from the sketchy reports of early observers. Dark sod lines, which indicate that it was not heaped up at one time, were exposed from time to time in the mound.(2) In addition to the many typically Adena log tombs found, were others which had been molded with puddled clay. In the tombs were mica and other more usual artifacts.(3) The Cincinnati Tablet was discovered by L. Wayne in a tomb at or near the center of the mound. When it was found, the roof of the tomb had not collapsed; the floor-to-roof dimension of two and one-half feet is strikingly close to the pit tombs recently excavated at the Sayler Park Mound. It is quite probable that we have here another example of the pit or bowl-shaped tombs which have been found in Adena Mounds throughout the Cincinnati area.(4)

The Cincinnati Tablet found in a Mound at Fifth and Mound Streets, Cincinnati

A second mound stood near the northeast corner of Seventh and Mound Streets (33-Ha.-225). It was flat-topped and nearly nine feet in height. "This (mound) has been penetrated to the center of its base without af-

---

(1) *Op. cit.*, Drake, Dr. Daniel

(2) Williams, John, *The American Pioneer*, Vol. II.

(3) *Op. cit.*, Clarke, p. 6.

(4) See Webb, Dr. Wm. S., *The Robbins Mounds*.

fording anything but some fragments of human skeletons, and a handful of copper beads which had been strung on a cord of lint . . . "(5)

A small mound (33-Ha.-221) on the east side of Central Avenue opposite Richmond Street was, when partially opened, found to contain "... a quantity of unfinished spear and arrowheads of flint."(6) Many such caches have been found in the Midwest, the most famous being that from the Hopewell site near Chillicothe; like other such finds, the one from Cincinnati is almost certainly attributable to the Hopewellian period.(7) Nine blocks further to the north was a "borrow pit" twelve feet in depth and fifty feet in diameter. No plausible explanation for this isolated phenomenon has been put forth.

Other less important mounds and village sites have been reported in the downtown basin as far north as Northside. Let it suffice to simply mention their former existence.

Two facts concerning the later historic Indian occupation of the Cincinnati plain will prove of importance in the later discussion of the Fort Finney Treaty. First, there were many Indian towns and villages on the low banks of the Ohio River prior to the disastrous flood of 1792 when the raging waters not only swept all the towns away, but also prompted the final removal of the aborigines from Hamilton County.(8) Secondly, there was a word (Tenlahahewhaghta) in the Wyandot language which designated the landing place at Cincinnati, but a similar word fails to appear in the Shawanoe (Shawnee) tongue. Of course, this might be due entirely to an oversight by the pioneer philologist, but that he was concerned with local place names is evident because he recorded Shawnee names for both the Great and Little Miami.(9) See next page.

ADDITIONAL MOUNDS AND VILLAGE SITES IN DELHI TOWNSHIP

From the basin area of Cincinnati to Sayler Park, nine miles down the Ohio, the river is closely confined by massive hills on both the Ohio and the Kentucky side, leaving but little low lying valley land and only a few terraces suitable for human occupation. Delhi Township does not offer much of archaeological interest in this river basin; with the exception of the Sayler Park-Fernbank plain there are only small Woodland villages and low mounds in this section of the valley.

The upland region of the township is primarily deeply eroded tableland which has probably never supported more than a scattering of Woodland camps. Of the six reported habitation sites, only one is still unspoiled by urban development. It is situated on a tongue of land a few hundred yards west of the end of Pedretti Avenue. The owner's collection

---

(5) *Op. cit.*, Drake, Dr. Daniel.

(6) *Ibid.*

(7) See Holmes Ellis's *The Possible Cultural Association of Flint Disk Caches*, in the Ohio State Archaeological and Historical Quarterly, Vol. XLIV, No. 2.

(8) See Harrison, William Henry: *A Discourse on the Aborigines of the Ohio Valley*, Fergus Printing Co., Chicago, 1883.

(9) Johnston, John Esq., *Account of the Present State of the Indian Tribes Inhabiting Ohio*, American Antiquarian Society, Vol. VI, pp. 298-297, Worcester, Massachusetts, 1819.

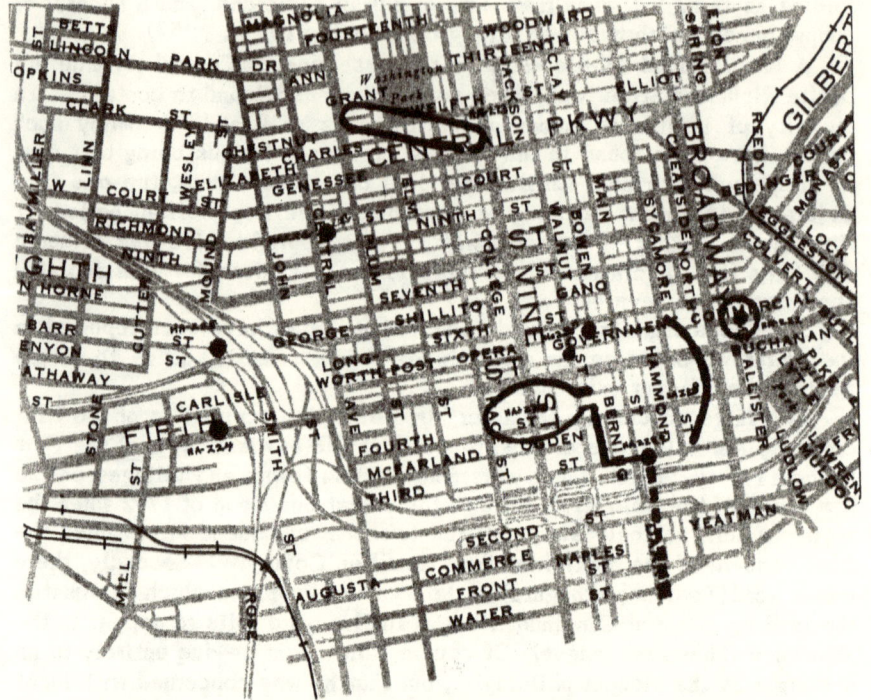

Map of Prehistoric Earthworks — the Site of Cincinnati

of hammerstones, cores, stemmed and side-notched points, and grooved axes typify the lithic culture represented there. Nearby, on the bluff west of Storrs Station, was a small mound which may still survive as an ancient monument indistinguishable from the group of low junk heaps which abound on the spot.

Another low tumulus crowns the bluff at Anderson Ferry. Three quarters of a mile west of the Anderson Ferry is a late Woodland site which has produced pottery reminiscent of the Newtown focus in Anderson Township (33-Ha.-12). The wide variety of projectile point types which occur at this site as well as the other components of the focus suggests that if a diagnostic shape exists for the Newtown points, it is as yet undiscovered. The only consistency readily discernible is the scarcity of specimens over two inches long.

Extending west of Mount St. Joseph on-the-Ohio is a long, elevated ridge on the end of which is the low St. Joseph Mound (33-Ha.-164). On the Kentucky hills opposite this point are three other tumuli, one of which stands out boldly on the profile of the hilltops and forms a striking sight from any vantage point on the Ohio side.

At Sayler Park the hills recede to form a level plain which was occupied not only by the builders of the earthwork mentioned above but also by other aborigines into the historic period. The principal Adena mound is the Sayler Park Mound (33-Ha.-157) which was recently excavated by the Cincinnati Museum of Natural History. The large eliptical tumulus contained thirty-nine burials, all but a few in tombs, numerous artifacts in association with these burials, the remains of two circular structures, and hundreds of Early Woodland sherds scattered throughout the fill. Of most aspects of the excavation of this mound little need be said here since a detailed account of the project is forthcoming and a summary report has already been published.[1]

From the pottery it seems possible that the mound is of fairly late Adena origin, a hypothesis which has been confirmed by the Carbon 14 date of approximately 2000 years.[2] It is hoped that tests on other specimens from the floor of the mound will give substantially earlier dates for the structures from which they were taken. In general though it can be said that the Sayler Park Mound fits safely into the "Late Adena" period recently defined by Baby and Webb.[3]

A partial list of traits from the mound would include:

I. Plan
   a) elliptical; 28 feet high; 175' x 140' base.

II. Inhumation technique
   a) unelaborated extended burials.
   b) simple log tombs
   c) multiple burials in log tombs
   d) pit or bowl-shaped tombs
   e) multiple burials in pit or bowl-shaped tombs

III. Non-ceramic Artifacts
   a) stemmed points
   b) drills, scrapers, etc.
   c) cache blades of Flint Ridge and Harrison Co. flint.
   d) fragment of grooved axe
   e) expanded center gorget
   f) copper bracelets and ring.
   g) cloth on three burials.
   h) tubular pipes: one bear effigy, one pottery.
   i) one duck effigy pipe

IV. Pottery
   a) limestone or grit tempered, cordmarked with plain or flaring lips and occasional incised decoration.
   b) Baumer type thick, rare.

V. Structures
   a) circular, 24 and 27 ft. in diameter.
   b) paired, or two posts in one hole type post molds.
   c) central post instead of hearth area.

---

[1] Starr, S. Frederick, *The Excavation of an Indian Mound in Sayler Park* in Hist. & Phil. Soc. of O. Bulletin, Vol. XVI., No. I.

[2] Test performed by the University of Michigan Memorial — Phoenix Project Radiocarbon Laboratory.

[3] See Webb, W. S.; and Baby, R.; *The Adena People* — No. 2, The Ohio Historical Society, Columbus, 1957, p. 112.

Log Tomb – Sayler Park Mound – Delhi Township

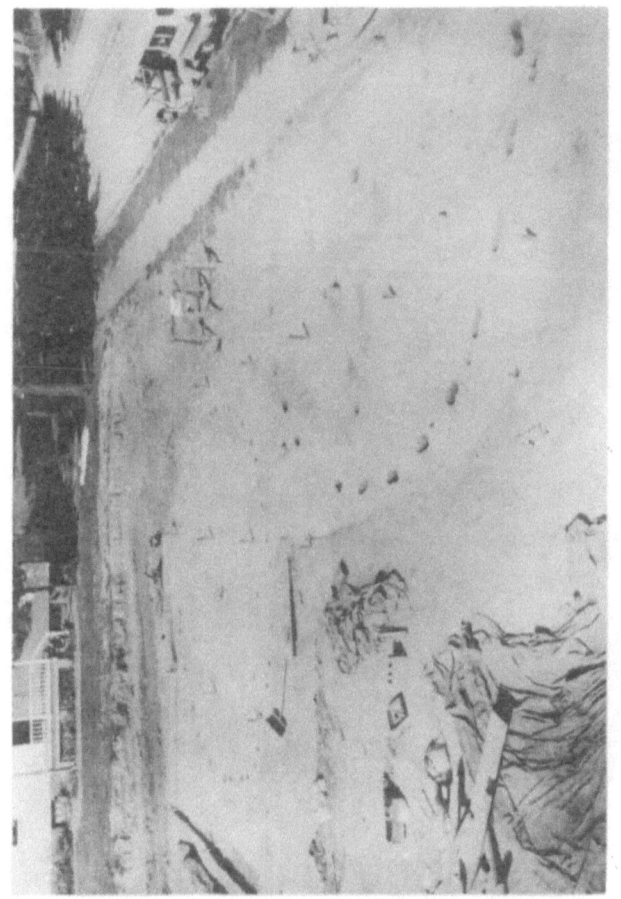

Structures I and II, Sayler Park Mound

Wall Angle of Structure I, Sayler Park Mound

Decorated Sherds - Limestone Tempered
Sayler Park Mound, Delhi Township

Rim Sherds from the Sayler Park Mound, Delhi Township

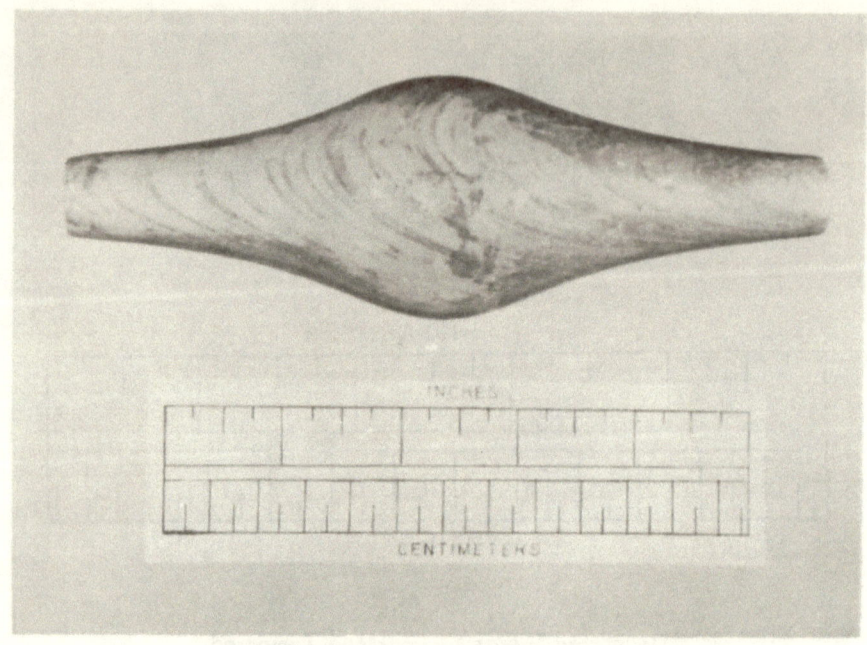

Expanded Center Gorget from Pit Tomb #1
Sayler Park Mound (33-Ha.-157)

Clay Bird Effigy Pipe
Pit Tomb #1, Sayler Park Mound

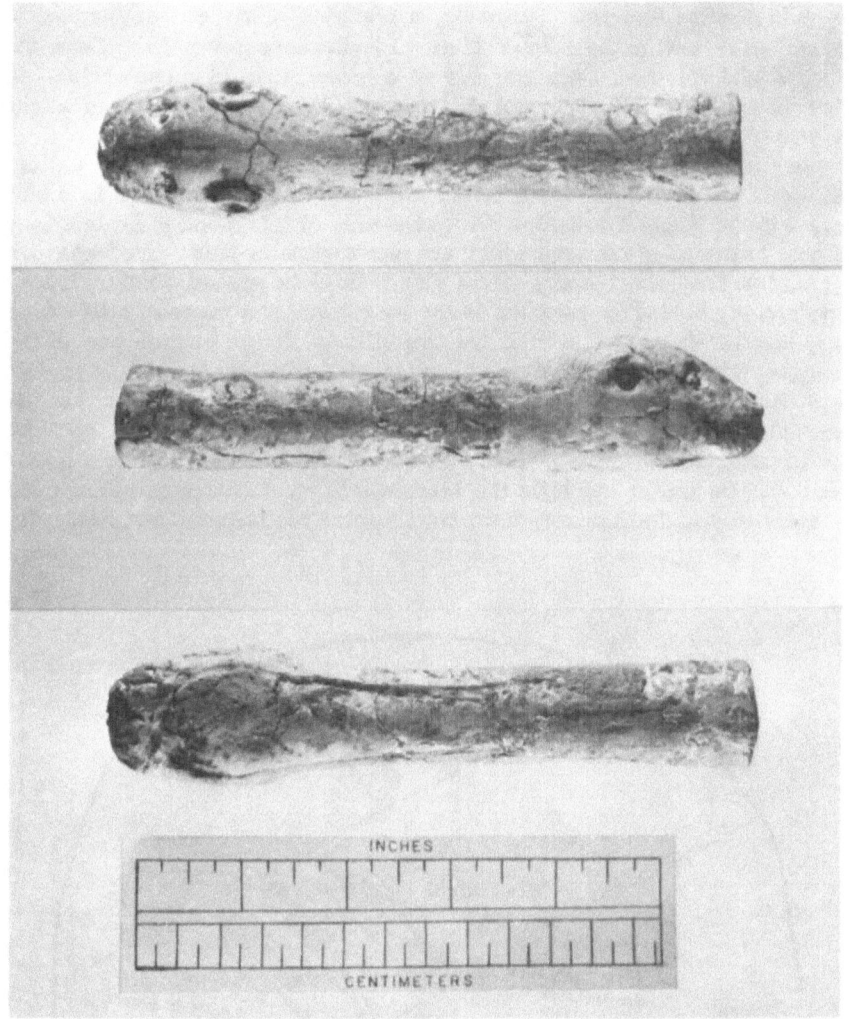

Bear Effigy Clay Tubular Pipe from the Sayler Park Mound

Another large mound still stands on the Shorts Woods Golf Course nearby. It too is elliptical (80' x 65') but only eight feet in height. (33-Ha.-13) Between these two tumuli at the end of Parkland Avenue is, according to local legend, the site of an historic Indian encampment. If the old story can be believed, the camp, located high above the bottoms on the edge of the terrace, was periodically occupied by Indians who often held wild celebrations there in the evenings. On the southernmost end of the same terrace above Gracely Drive, is a low mound three feet in height and forty feet in diameter. (33-Ha.-14)

ADDITIONAL MOUNDS AND VILLAGE SITES IN MIAMI TOWNSHIP

Miami Township occupies the same position relative to the Great Miami River as Anderson Township does to the Little Miami. Although not as large in area as Anderson Township, it contains nearly as many archaeological sites and gains further distinction because fewer have been destroyed and the ones remaining are in a better state of preservation. In view of the natural features of the township, one is not surprised at the volume of its archaeological wealth.

In the many centuries of its twisting and winding through its valley, the Great Miami has formed a level, low-lying flood plain which is a half mile wide in Miami Township. On either side of this flood plain is a long terrace or series of terraces which are elevated about thirty-five feet above the bottom land and thereby afford safety from the annual floods. Rising very steeply behind the terraces is the long, triangular range of hills which separate the Miami Valley from the Ohio River. In the eastern part of the triangle, where it connects to the mass of eroded land which stretches from Cincinnati to North Bend, the drop to the valley is steep, but not impassable. However, as one progresses out toward the western point of the triangle, the hills, especially on the Ohio River side, become nearly vertical. On top of the hills the land is rolling, dotted with springs and in every way fit for human habitation; likewise the terraces and lowlands,

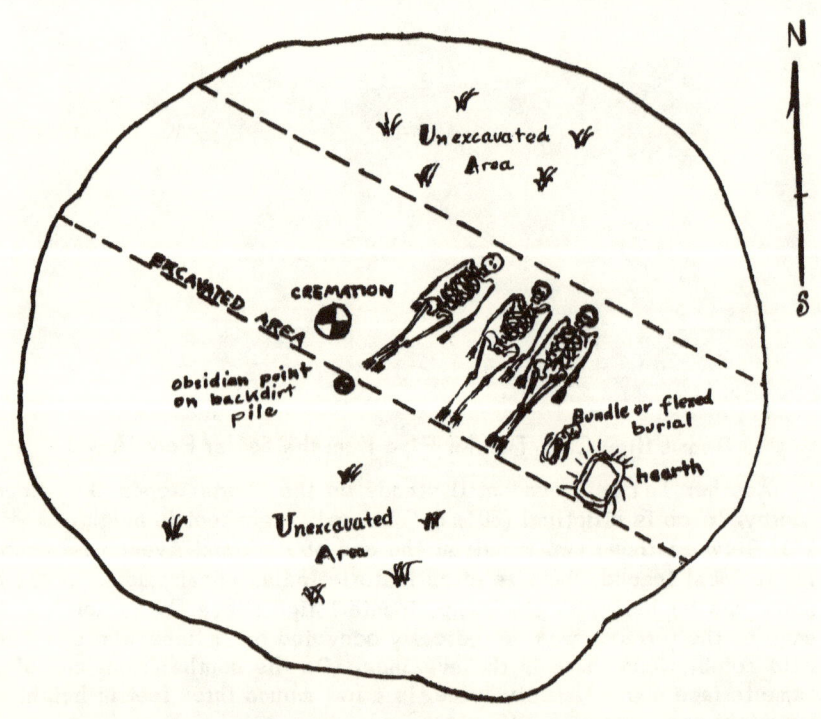

Shinkal Mound (33-Ha.-87)
Miami Township

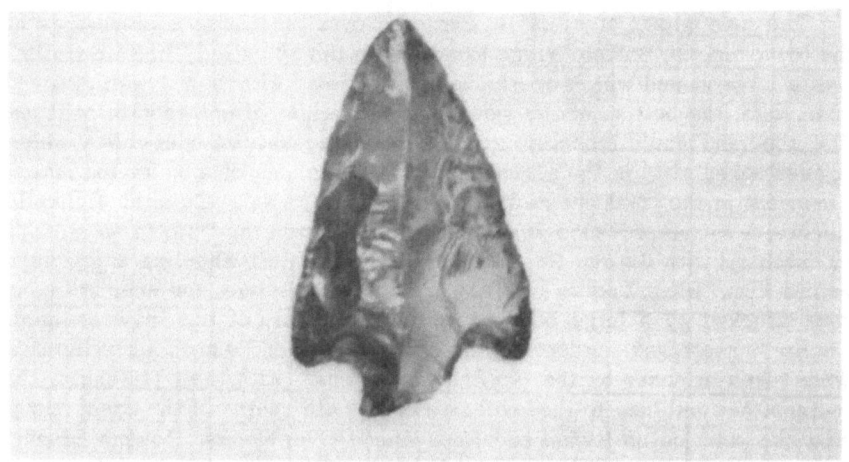

Obsidian Point from Shinkal Mound (33-Ha.-87) Miami Township
(Fitzpatrick Collection)

with their easy access to the rivers, met the needs of numerous prehistoric communities. Nowhere else in Hamilton County are there so many types of topography represented in such a small area.

The first group of sites is in the eastern part of the township near the Township School on Bridgetown Road. Exactly opposite the school was a mound (33-Ha.-85) which was removed in 1958 to make way for a new sub-division. It was twelve feet high, had a diameter of about seventy feet and was composed of topsoil. At various spots throughout the mound were areas in which concentrations of charcoal and burnt rock appeared. Forty yards to the south was a borrow pit, part of which was still clearly visible when the survey visited the site. According to local sources the pit was once nearly eight feet in depth and sixty feet in diameter. Nearby is a village site (33-Ha.-86); four polished celts, two corner notched points, one side notched point, hammerstones, cores and three Flint Ridge flake knives taken from this site are in the Fitzpatrick collection.

A mile or so northeast from the above village is a major Hopewell mound which was partially excavated by a group of untrained amateurs in 1952. Judging from the portion which still remains, it seems likely that it was about four feet in height and two hundred-fifty feet in circumference. The trench which was dug through the center of the tumulus encountered three extended burials placed next to each other and one foot apart. Adjacent to the feet of one skeleton, there was evidence of a cremation, i.e. small fragments of burnt bone in a pile. A few feet on the other side of the group was what seems to have been either a bundle burial or tightly flexed inhumation. Next to and beneath the last skeleton was a hearth-like clay formation which was possibly a crematory basin. Only one artifact was found, it being a small, stemmed projectile point made from obsidian. This artifact of an unusual type occurs in the Illinois branch of the Hopewell culture but is quite rare in Ohio. Whether or not it had originally been placed with one of the burials is not known.

The next group of sites is scattered over the entire eastern area of the township. On Buffalo Ridge Road, above the so-called "buffalo trails" was a large mound which overlooked the valley. Although it was removed years ago, the bottom of the mound, to the height of one foot is still undisturbed and would probably reward careful excavation. The valley which it overlooked was, in the summer of 1781, the scene of a major Indian encampment in the final phase of the Revolutionary War. Colonel Archibald Lochry, a native of Pennsylvania, had sailed down the Ohio in an attempt to catch up with George Rogers Clark, who had left Wheeling a few days before him. When Lochry reached a point near Aurora, Indiana, his army was attacked by a large band of Indians, probably of the Shawnee race. Lochry himself was murdered as he sat on a log, and sixty-four of his men were taken prisoner by the pro-British Indians. With their prisoners, the Indians then returned to the level area on the old course of the Great Miami near the junction of Jordon and East Miami River Roads. Joseph Brandt, the renowned Indian statesman, and George Girty, the despised American turncoat, retained their force at that campsite until four hundred additional Indians and British arrived as reinforcements. With the newly swelled forces, camp was broken and a march begun down the Ohio in an attempt to overtake and destroy George Rogers Clark's army.[1] The later American decision to remove the Shawnee nation from Hamilton County was undoubtedly due in large part to their counter-revolutionary activities of 1781. A reminder of this powerful British-Indian campaign against the revolutionaries is the brass regimental medallion which was found near the mouth of the Miami by Charles B. Winter.

Taylor High School in North Bend is built over the site of an archaic village. The number of burials which were found when the school was built, and the material in many local collections testify to the richness of the site. Although the skeletons were not saved, the stemmed points, drilled shell disks, rough pestles and bannerstones are all typical archaic artifacts.

The high hill above Cleves on Mt. Nebo Road is crowned with three tumuli (33-Ha.-28, 97, 29). The first is situated on a tapering, level promontory about fifty yards from the road. It seems to be made of stone and dirt, but the dense vegetation on it prohibited accurate observation. The second of the group was recently removed; it stood on the edge of the bluff above Cleves. On the highest point of the Suit property is a three foot high mound-like projection. Its location as well as its appearance suggest that it is not of natural origin.

Three quarters of a mile to the southwest are the two Rittenhouse sites. One, a campsite, is located near the corner of Rittenhouse and Mt. Nebo Roads and the other, a village site, is on the high hilltop immediately to the southwest. Both have yielded scores of lithic artifacts, but to date, no pottery. Although beautifully polished banded slate objects

---

[1] Maurer, C. J., *The British Version of Lochry's Defeat;* Bulletin, Historical and Philosophical Society of Ohio, Vol. 10, No. 3, pp. 215-229.

have been found from time to time on both sites, prosaic celts, stemmed points, chisels, and scrapers are more representative.

The last and largest group of sites are all located within one and three-quarters mile of the confluence of the Miami and Ohio Rivers. It is at this place that the triangular range of hills forms the corner upon which Miami Fort and the Point Stone Mound were built. By far the largest number of villages, however, were located not on the hilltop, but in the valley below.

In describing these sites, we shall begin at the terrace at the foot of the "point" where a concentration of Archaic artifacts has been found (33-Ha.-136). Signs of the most intensive occupation are seen, especially around the lip of a depression from which a spring once flowed, but the entire area is strewn with flint, etc.

Before moving to the next village, it would be well to note a little known but colorful event which occurred near here. The incident is the claiming of the region by the French and it took place in August, 1749. A typically romantic nineteenth century description best suits the character of the event:

> "At the mouth of La Riviere a la Roche, as the French then called the Great Miami, Celeron moored his little navy of birchbark canoes and with courtly and dramatic ceremonies planted his last lead plate, proclaiming that these rivers and all their tributaries belonged to his majesty, Louis (XV), King of France."(2)

Similar plates were buried at the mouths of the Muskingum, Wabash and other rivers in the Midwest. However, since the Miami has changed its course so frequently in the past one hundred and fifty years, it seems highly improbable that this fascinating relic of French rule will ever be found.

The DuPont Corporation has recently built a plant a few hundred yards to the east of the above village. As soon as the ground had been broken it was immediately evident that one of the major Archaic village sites in Southwestern Ohio had been found (33-Ha.-11). Archaic people were living in the Hamilton County area by at least five-hundred years B.C. and most likely many centuries earlier. This village occupied the level end of a knoll which spread for about three acres along an east-west line between Brower Road and the railroad tracks. The entire area has been deeply eroded, causing the naturally rolling land to appear much more rugged than it was only forty years ago. Four extended burials were removed by collectors from the eroding bank of the hillside. Standing on the railroad tracks, one can still see the crescent shaped outlines of fireplaces on the cross section.

The largest part of the site was covered with unstratified Archaic material. Stone mortars and cup-stones have been found; flint artifacts in-

---

(2) Randall, E. O., *Masterpieces of the Mound Builders*, Ohio State Archaeological and Historical Society, Columbus, 1908, p. 56.

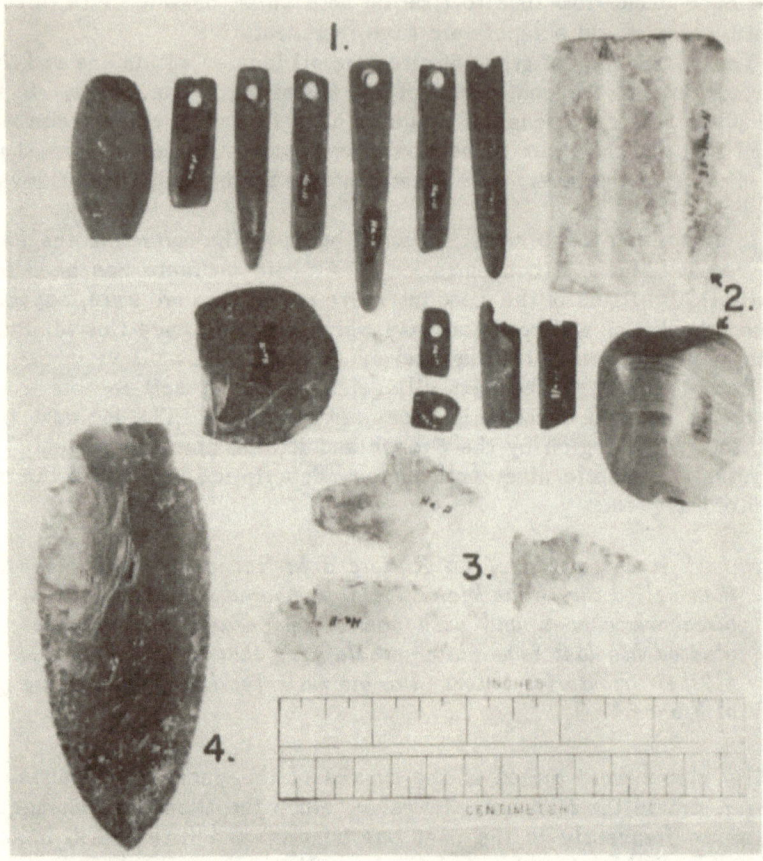

Archaic Artifacts from the DuPont Site, 33-Ha.-11, Miami Township.
1) Cannel Coal Pendants and bead.
2) Banner Stones: above — quartsite
   below — banded slate.
3) Chert projectile points.
4) Dark flint blade.

clude small-stemmed projectile points, drills and scrapers; shells were worked into rather large beads and slate was used for bannerstones and other artifacts of unknown function. The many uses to which cannel coal was put, and the volume of it found at the DuPont Site, indicate that a readily accessible source of the material existed. In addition to those objects shown in the accompanying picture is a very unusual cannel coal plummet in the C. B. Winter collection. Although much was learned by the brief visits of the Cincinnati Museum of Natural History and the Ohio State Museum to the DuPont site, valuable architectural, domestic and funerary data on the Archaic period have been irretrievably lost here.

Before the railroad came to North Bend, the field which contained the DuPont site formed the back yard of the Harrison home, residence of two presidents. An outbuilding in which the hired help lived stood on the levelled top of a mound behind the old brick farmhouse. From the early nineteenth century, when it was first levelled down, until 1910 when it was finally removed for the railroad right-of-way, the mound was six feet high. C. B. Winter, who removed the tumulus, recalls finding "at least one burial" and both grooved axes and chisels in it. Recently, a crude fragment of a granite pop-eyed birdstone was found a few rods east of the Harrison home near the Fort Finney Monument.

Fort Finney, the first American military outpost in the region, was located in the vicinity of the Harrison home. This fort, or multiple blockhouse, was built especially for the negotiation of a treaty which was made between " . . . the Commissioners Plenipotentiary of the United States and the Chiefs and Warriors of the Shawanoe Nation,"[3] in January, 1786. This was the seventh Indian treaty negotiated by the newly formed United States. An examination of the document reveals several interesting points.

It is divided into seven articles, the first of which provides that the Indians deliver three hostages to be held until all of the Americans who had been taken prisoner during the fighting were returned to representatives of the United States. In the second article the Shawanoes acknowledged the United States to be "the sole and absolute sovereign of all the territory ceded to them by (the Anglo-American treaty of 1784)."[4] In return for "friendship and protection" the Indians agreed to deliver up criminals and to report all plots against the United States which should come to their attention. Articles six and seven assure territorial integrity to both negotiating parties – the line between them being the Great Miami River. Americans who either settled or caused disturbance on the western side would lose the protection of the United States, while Shawanoes relinquished "all title or pretence they ever had"[5] to land outside their reservation.

From the general tone of the treaty it is obvious that the Americans, led by George Rogers Clark, completely dominated the session. In all probability, the Americans, as victors, had taken more prisoners than had the Indians, but no provisions are made for their return to the Shawanoe Nation. Moreover, eight Shawnees as opposed to only three Americans, were required to sign the pact. To learn the later effects of the treaty on the lives of the Shawanoes, we must look to the Fort Harmar Treaty which was made three years after the Fort Finney Treaty at the American outpost on the Muskingum River. In that treaty between the Wyandots and the Americans, the fate of the Shawanoe Nation is mentioned:

"Be it remembered, that the Wyandots have laid claim to the lands that were granted to the Shawanese, at the treaty held at the Miami, and have declared, that as the Shawanese have been so restless, and caused so much trouble, both to

---

[3] Kapler, Charles J., *Indian Affairs, Laws and Treaties*, Washington, 1904, p. 16, 17.
[4] *Ibid.*, p. 17.
[5] *Ibid.*, p. 17.

them and to the United States, if they will not now be at peace, they will dispossess them, and take the country into their own hands; for that the country is theirs of right, and the Shawanese are only living upon it by their permission. They further lay claim to all the country west of the Miami boundary, from the village to the lake Erie, and declare that it is now under their management and direction."(6)

The restlessness mentioned existed both before and after the Fort Finney Treaty. An American who was present at the council wrote that over two months were consumed in persuading the Shawnees to come to the meeting,(7) and later, while the Harmar Treaty was being written, a band of Shawnees massacred a group of surveyors from Ft. Washington who were working in western Hamilton County.

That the Wyandots gained the upper hand in that Shawanoe area is shown by the fact that no Shawnees were found by the earliest white settlers who named Wyandot Creek in the center of the Shawanoe territory. Likewise, it can be said that the numerous Indian towns which were swept from the banks of the Ohio in 1792 were definitely not occupied by Shawnees, but probably by Wyandots. Archaeological remains of the warlike Shawnee are suggested by the "towns" (note plural) which are mentioned repeatedly in the Ft. Finney Treaty. Some of these were doubtlessly in what is now Miami Township. These would have been abandoned after the treaty of 1786; the remainder and probably the majority were in Indiana, or in Whitewater, Harrison and Crosby Townships in Ohio.

Many cannonballs, buttons and other relics have been found on the Ohio River terraces near the site of Fort Finney, the most dense concentration of both historical relics and prehistoric artifacts being at the Harrison village site (33-Ha.-10). Only the Hopewellian artifacts from the site require our attention since the historical relics are not as yet associated with specific European peoples. The Indian artifacts include both grit and limestone tempered sherds, the former equally divided between cordmarked and plain; long, stemmed projectile points; drop shaped blades; celts and the usual village lithic material and debris. Fragments of a burial were found by the survey in the bottom of a nearby irrigation ditch and others are reported to have been found in the riverbank a few dozen yards distant from the site.

Between the center of the Harrison Site and the Columbia Power Plant were recently found a number of hearths, similar in all respects to those discussed below (p. 113). Although at least six fully grooved pecked and polished axes were found nearby but not in a position which would suggest a relationship. Rather, these hearths seem to have no artifacts with them at all.

---

(6) *Ibid.*, p. 22.

(7) Abbott, John S. C., *History of Ohio*, Tyler and Co., Detroit, 1875, p. 419.

(8) *Ibid.*, p. 317.

East of Mound Avenue and south of Brower Road is a level area on which travelling groups of Indians often camped in the early 1800s and where a detachment of soldiers camped during the Civil War. Local tradition insists that the Indians were often quite raucous and, in payment to the owner for his patience, would give him a trinket. Half of a mound still remains in Dark Hollow on the American Bituminous Company's property. Another, eight feet in height, was destroyed when the oil tanks were built. (33-Ha.-107) C. B. Winter describes it as being about one-hundred ninety feet in circumference and made entirely of gravel which had evidently been carried from an outcropping to the west. Running in a northeast-southwest line through the center of the tumulus was a low wall laid with flat sedimentary rocks. Covering the wall in many spots was a "tarlike substance" of unknown identity. Until further work is done in the Miami Township area, it would be fruitless to guess as to the origin of this mound or the identity of the "tarlike substance".

Still further east, on the narrow terrace where the Ohio River sweeps close to the hills is a little-known village site. At the time the survey visited the site, surface conditions were such that collecting was impossible, but the eroding bank of the stream which delineates the site showed a thin stratum of dark midden. Two burials were salvaged from this bank by C. B. Winter whose excellent collection contains many side-notched points from the surface.

Moving now to the rolling hills high above the last site, we come to a group of mounds on the Cincinnati Gas and Electric Company's property. All located within one and one-half miles of each other, they are to be found on practically every level spot on the hilltop. The first is on the edge of the bluff and, considering its exposed location, is very well preserved. It is about ten feet high and of the conical type. (33-Ha.-108) This mound is a few dozen yards from the top of an old road which winds up the hillside through a creek bed. Eighty yards southwest of the road is a smaller companion to the first mound. The dense growth of underbrush on it prohibits accurate measurement but its height appears to be about two feet and, unlike the other mounds in the group, it has an eliptical base rather than a round one, the longer dimension corresponding to the orientation of spur of the hill upon which it is located. (33-Ha.-109)

Looking across the wider angle formed by that spur, one sees an acre of level land fairly isolated by the shallow ravines on its peripheries. On the northern side of this elevation is a tumulus which, judging from the flake knives which have been found near it, is of Hopewellian origin. (33-Ha.-110) The years of exposure and annual plowing which it once suffered have caused its diameter to spread to over one hundred feet and its height to be reduced to seven feet, barely half of its original height. The earthwork-like elevation along the edge of the precipice is most likely the grass-grown edge of an old plow furrow.

Further toward Miami Fort are three more mounds, two of which are barely discernible in the open field, the third being seven feet in height and grown over with large forest trees. The first two are of interest because of their possible relation to a fourth mound which once stood near to them. Years ago, when it was dug into, a pipe, decorated with the effigy of a human face, was found. The present whereabouts of this artifact is unknown. The third mound is situated on a slight projection from which the Great Miami Valley is visible. (33-Ha.-111, 112, 113)

Just beyond the above group, the hilltop narrows to form an isthmus between the main body of the triangle and Miami Fort. On this narrow strip is the most important Hopewell village site in the county. (33-Ha.-24) It is best described by the material which it has yielded:

        3 flake knives
      12 cores
      17 rough points or blanks
      15 scrapers
       5 long thin Woodland blades (2½-3½'')
       8 stemmed points
       1 large triangular base
       3 small unstemmed points
      12 broken points
       6 side-notched points
       1 corner-notched point
       1 Fort Ancient triangular point
       2 polished celts
       1 end of polled celt
       2 unfinished celts
       3 grooved axes(**)
       1 seventeen inch roller pestle(**)
       1 cup stone
       1 slate hoe
        shells, antlers and broken animal bones
Pottery — limestone tempered
          23 cordmarked
          94 smooth
           3 rims
    — grit tempered
          38 cordmarked
          38 smooth
           1 finely tempered dentate-stamped sherd
           4 rims
        one large piece of unformed pottery or daub

(**) Artifacts in the C. B. Winter collection

Parts of two burials were recovered by the survey. These constitute two of the three known Hopewell village burials from the county. The third, from a nearby site, is described below. The two interments just mentioned were found within forty feet of the Twin Mounds, two large tumuli placed next to each other on one side of the village. Their topographical location is very much like the five conjoined mounds in Anderson Township. (33-Ha.-182) Unfortunately, these mounds too have been deeply scarred by amateur collectors.

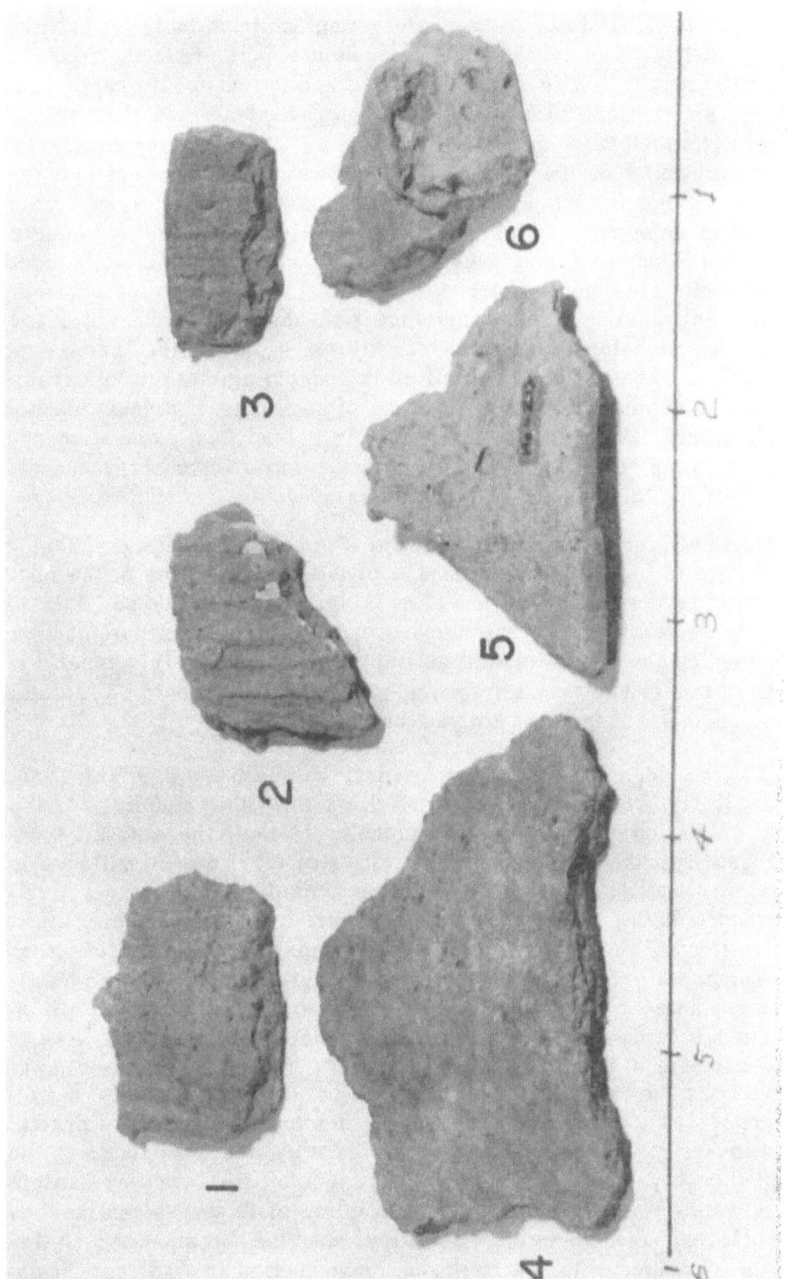

Sherds from Twin Mounds Village, 33-Ha.-24
1, 2 – Cordmarked, limestone tempered. 3, 5, 6 – Rims. 4 – Dentate Stamped, fine grit tempered.

The elevated, exposed, yet isolated site which was chosen by the builders of the Twin Mounds and village is a potential clue to the discovery of the exact purpose of the Hopewellian hilltop earthworks or forts. Briefly, the opposing views in this interesting and important, yet baffling archaeological problem are these: some scholars, pointing to the frequent failure of Indians to fortify strategic points and the obviously ceremonial nature of certain finds at Fort Ancient, etc., contend that the "forts" were not constructed for defensive purposes. Others, citing such well planned earthworks as the Clark's Work or Miami Fort, contend that the utilization of high isolated hilltops could not have been for any other purpose than defense. In light of the alternatives, one should observe that the Twin Mounds village, largest of the communities which surrounded the earthwork, does not answer the primitive need for protection from elements. Added to that is its distance from the rivers from which the mussels (and probably fish) which constituted a part of the Indian diet were obtained. Whether one is justified in concluding that the inconvenience of access was accepted in the face of necessity of defense cannot yet be decided. Until more precise data is gained from excavation and Carbon 14 dating, the whole problem of the purpose, chronology and development of the hilltop "forts" will remain a mystery.

Pottery similar to that found at the Twin Mounds Village and the Harrison Site is found also on a number of the small terraces at the base of the fort on the Great Miami Valley side. Actually, these plots of ground are sections of the long narrow terrace which are separated from one another by the deeply eroded gullies between them. This results in a series of one or two acre terraces upon which people could be isolated from one another and from the bottoms below.

Below the ridge leading to the "Point" of Miami Fort is 33-Ha.-64, a Hopewell site covering one acre. Neither the lithic material nor the ceramic collection is in any way unusual. In fact, the ceramic type-percentages from this site are representative of all Hopewell villages in the western Hamilton County area. Grit tempered ware comprises sixty-five per cent of the total, the remaining thirty-five per cent being limestone tempered. The grit is either fine or medium coarse, and often includes quartz while medium coarse limestone particles are found in nearly all of the others. Of the grit tempered sherds, fifty per cent are plain, all others are cordmarked. The limestone tempered ware breaks down to seventy per cent plain and only thirty per cent cordmarked. The shapes of the vessels cannot be reconstructed from the diminutive sherds, but all of the rims found thus far are straight, unexpanded and undecorated. Neither rocker stamped nor ornate inscribed ware has been found in the village; the only unusual sherd is a fragment of grit tempered dentate stamped ware. When a more thorough sampling of larger specimens has been collected, the Hopewellian pottery from the Great Miami Valley should be compared with the Newtown Focus series in Anderson Township, for many aspects of these two Woodland cultures are so much alike that a direct connection may have existed. Indeed this relationship has been pointed out by Edward V. McMichael:

"Newtown postdates classic Hopewell, and with little doubt is derived from it, in the form of a decline after the climax. One may easily characterize the Newtown focus as 'Hopewellian,' with the elaborations missing."(9)

For the most part, the "elaborations" seem to be missing even on the "classic" Hopewell villages of the Miami Fort area.

Continuing to the next division of the terrace we come to another small, concentrated Hopewell village. Unlike the preceding site, both Fort Ancient and Archaic artifacts occur here. The Fort Ancient period is represented by five shell tempered Madisonville plain sherds. Mr. George Hayhurst has a discoidal, two adzes, four Flint Ridge flake knives, a flint hoe and one banded slate bannerstone. Two crude expanded center gorgets, one in the Winter collection and the other in the Hayhurst collection are identical to specimens from the Woodland level of the Turpin site. The adzes and bannerstone are probably Archaic artifacts, as is the large curved pick shaped bannerstone which was found years ago by one of the present owner's children. After being rented to collectors for use in exhibitions it was sold to a private collection in Indiana where it is today.

In the summer of 1958 a new home was built on a terrace further to the northeast. While the basement was being excavated at least one burial was found. After the cut was completed a thirty inch thick mantle of dark midden was exposed. Since the owner forbade all collecting, salvage digging and even photographing we have no precise knowledge as to its cultural affinity. Local collectors group it with the Miami Fort Hopewell.

The Zeigler farm, located on a large terrace above Brower Road, contains the site of a Woodland village. It has yielded many projectile points, celts, etc. but only a few fragments of limestone tempered pottery. A more productive site is the Stoneking village near the corner of Dugan Gap and Brower Roads. (33-Ha.-60) At this point the terrace is level and forty yards wide but the cultural material is crowded on the few yards nearest to the hill. The artifacts found by the survey were:

              1 hammerstone
              2 celts
              1 side-notched base
              1 triangular base
              3 leaf shaped blades
              4 proj. point fragments
Pottery — grit tempered
              8 cordmarked
             10 plain
       — shell tempered
              2 cordmarked
            18 plain
              1 decorated rim

---

(9)McMichael, Edward V., From "The Newtown Focus"; read at the Twenty-second Annual Meeting of the S. A. A.; May, 1957, Madison, Wisconsin.

The grit tempered pottery is coarser than most of the sherds from neighboring sites but the Fort Ancient group is entirely of the common Madisonville type.

The final group of sites in the township is concentrated on the level plain which runs from the end of Mt. Nebo Road to well beyond the large gravel pits one-half mile to the northeast. Since habitational evidence covers the entire area, the division into separate sites is based on the relative concentrations. In the far corner of the field south of Mt. Nebo Road is a concentration of Woodland material. This village covered two acres and was bordered on the east by a small stream. In the same relative position to the north of the road and conforming to the limits of a one hundred yard long knoll is an Archaic village site. (33-Ha.-66) Although no ground stone artifacts have been found as yet, the many flint scrapers and points are identical to those from the DuPont site. Southeast of an imaginary line between these two villages is a conical mound forty feet in diameter and one foot in height. Both plowing and intentional grading have reduced it to its present size.

A much larger tumulus was one of four archaeological sites destroyed when the gravel pits were dug. One hundred yards from it were two others which were aligned east to west and, according to Mr. Tony Collins, of Hooven, Ohio, were "practically touching one another". Between the large mound, which was six feet high, and the other two, which were both about four feet in elevation, was a village where Mr. Ratterman found an extended burial three feet below the surface. (33-Ha.-263) Thin sheets of mica covered the entire skeleton. The Collins collection contains grooved axes, celts, roller pestles, bell pestles, stemmed projectile points and a heavy tubular slate pipe from the site. The projectile points and tubular pipes would usually be classified as Adena artifacts while the mica covering on the burial is a Hopewellian trait. Obviously the Hopewell-Adena relationship needs further study to fully explain this phenomenon.

ADDITIONAL MOUNDS AND VILLAGE SITES IN GREEN AND COLERAIN TOWNSHIPS

Green Township is north of Delhi Township and east of Miami Township; it extends from the Great Miami River on the west to Cincinnati on the east. Directly north of Green Township is Colerain Township which is bordered on the north by Butler County, on the east by Springfield Township and on the west by the Great Miami River. As it flows past Colerain Township the river forms the broad flat plain upon which the Colerain Earthwork is located, but from that wide point the valley narrows until the river nearly washes the sides of the high hills on either bank. Archaeologically, Green Township and that part of Colerain which it borders is practically sterile. The uneven terrain which characterizes most of the area is ill suited to the needs of all but the most rudimentary hunting cultures. That pre-Columbian Indians frequented the region is attested by the countless random field finds which glut the many local collections, but the survey was able to prove the existence of only two small campsites. Due to the paucity of sites, most of Green Township was ignored and attention was turned to the valley area of Colerain Township.

On a terrace above Ripple Road near Harrison Pike is part of a large Woodland village. (33-Ha.-88) Today the Stitle Site is only seventy-five feet square but prior to the gravelling operations on its eastern side it covered over two acres. The terrace occupies the same commanding position in respect to the valley below as do those near Miami Fort and the four sherds found, all limestone tempered, are quite like the Miami Fort ware. The survey's collection consists of one side-notched point, two stemmed points, one Woodland leaf blade, four broken points, one grooved axe, and the four pieces of limestone tempered, cordmarked pottery. The Stitles, who own the site, once had "a bushel full" of artifacts which were found when the gravel pits were opened. Further north in the valley on the Louis Flick farm at Flick and Blue Rock Roads is another high terrace which was intensively inhabited. (33-Ha.-81) It is surrounded on three sides by tributaries of Blue Rock Creek and on the fourth by the hill behind. Mr. Edward Schneider of Cheviot has a large collection from here which is unusual in the high percentage of artifacts made from Harrison County, Indiana, flint.

Unpolished celts, stemmed points, and Harrison County flint flakes, together with the usual cores and stones were found on the lower land along Blue Rock Creek near East Miami River Road. The occupation zone is confined to a barely traceable rise in the otherwise flat field. West of East Miami River Road and across from the State Conservation Bureau's farm is a village site which covers three-quarters of an acre. Since the field was fallow at the time of the survey's visit, only a polished celt, a few stemmed points and flakes were found.

On the hill above the Colerain Earthwork known locally as Bowling Green is a large village site and, on the next hill to the south, a little-known mound. The County History of 1881 mentions this as being one of the most prolific prehistoric villages in the area and many of the old Miami valley residents confirm that epithet with reports of finding dozens of corner notched blades as long as one's hand. After years of plowing and collecting, only the usual debris remains on the surface, but an unusually deep plowing never fails to turn up a few new artifacts.

Directly below Bowling Green is the site of Dunlap's Station, one of the chain of outposts built in Hamilton County at the end of the eighteenth century. This peaceful spot, in 1790, was witness to a bloody Indian raid. The band of attacking Indians was composed of Miamis, Delawares, Shawnees, and a few "Puttawatamies." Inside the fort, Lieutenant Jacob Kingsbury and his garrison of thirty-five regulars fortified themselves and the civilians as best they could against the renowned Little Turtle's force of three hundred.[1] We know that at the end of the twenty-four hour siege, at least ten Indians were dead and the same number wounded. Two Americans were killed in battle, and a third

---

[1] Beckwith, Hiram W., *A Treatise on the Western Indians*, Fergus Printing Co., Chicago, 1883, p. 83.

was murdered amid the destroyed outbuildings within sight of the defenders. The importance of this incident lies in the fact that as late as 1790 at least some Shawnees were still fighting to regain the land they signed away at Fort Finney.

Directly south of Bowling Green and across Dunlap Road is a very precipitous hill on the top of which is a conical tumulus ten feet high and sixty feet in diameter. Shortly after the turn of the century, a cistern was built into the apex of the mound to a depth of six feet, but if anything was found while it was being dug it was not recorded.

Along the hills stretching from Bowling Green across the northern part of the township is a group of small village sites which have both grit and limestone tempered pottery, celts and grooved axes, and varied projectile point types as common traits. Typical of the group is the Hunter site which is on the hill just west of Jackson Road and straddling the Butler county line. The sherds are all grit and limestone tempered, but are so badly weathered that their surface finish is indeterminable. Although both celts and fully grooved axes are reported from the site, further collection by the survey was impossible due to the presence of a wheat crop on the site.

ADDITIONAL MOUNDS AND VILLAGE SITES IN CROSBY TOWNSHIP

Crosby Township is on the northern border of the county across the Great Miami River from Colerain Township. Excepting the uneven eastern boundary, it is roughly rectangular in shape and covers an area of about fifteen square miles; the terrain is characterized by a flat to rolling plain broken by ranges of high hills. Besides the Great Miami, Dry Run, and Howard Creek, abundant springs and small creeks provided an ample water supply for the many prehistoric inhabitants of the township.

A very interesting concentration of sites is to be found on the land around Fernald in the northeastern quarter of the township. The first of these is a mound which stands on the brink of a seven hundred and ten foot high hill a few hundred yards west of the center of Fernald on the New Haven road. The tumulus (33-Ha.-128) is slightly elliptical now — the length difference between its north-south and its east-west axes is nine feet — but was most likely of the conical form originally. In its present state it is five and one half feet high. In addition to the natural erosion which has taken place, a hole was dug into its top by a Mr. Haehurst of Fernald who found nothing.

Nearby is a small habitation site which was occupied by an early preceramic people. (33-Ha.-130) This campsite was discovered by a resident of Fernald who encountered ashes and hearths while digging post-holes. The only artifact definitely attributable to the site is a beautiful butterfly bannerstone which was found among the ashes and is now in the Haehurst collection. It is made from banded slate and is highly polished. The grain was carefully utilized by the craftsman to produce not only a strong tool but the most artistically pleasing symmetry. The length of the hole drilled through the center of the oval artifact is three and one half inches. A straight sided lancelate point with basal grinding extending half way up the sides was found either at this site or at the Campbell site in the valley to the east.

The Campbell site (33-Ha.-127) is southwest of the corner of State Route 128 and the New Haven Road. The owner has found pecked and polished celts, drills and Archaic arrow heads in the sandy topsoil. One of the forked-base type points has also been found. These generally occur on Late Woodland villages.

Early settlers in the Great Miami valley often noted in their papers that a chain of "lookout mounds" ran from the mouth of the river for many miles up the valley. According to their reports, by standing on the top of one, one was able to see to the next one, from which the next one was visible, etc. Late nineteenth century chroniclers imagined that the chain somehow crossed into the Little Miami valley and thus connected Miami Fort with Fort Ancient, near Lebanon, Ohio, forty-three miles away. One of the two remaining tumuli of the chain is the Fox Mound near Paddy's Run Road north of Fernald. (33-Ha.-129) It is of regular shape, three and one-half feet high and sixty-nine feet in diameter. From the top of this "lookout mound" it is barely possible to see the next field, much less the next link in the "chain" of mounds.

Two and one half miles southeast of the small village of New Haven in the low floodland of the Great Miami River is "Whipple's Burying Ground", a prehistoric cemetery in which the graves were "marked by stones."[1] It is difficult to identify the exact position of this site since the river's course has changed repeatedly in the last three-quarter century.

About two-thirds of a mile south of New Haven on the high range of hills which overlooks the Miami valley was a cemetery and two mounds. According to the 1881 History of Hamilton, over fifty graves were exhumed at this cemetery in the eighteen fifties. At the foot of the hill upon which these three cities are situated is a small campsite which covers the field in the corner of Mount Hope Road above the Miami-Whitewater Forest. The quantity of lithic material, coupled with the paucity of other artifacts and debris would place this site in the nineteenth century classification of attelier, or workshop.

Above New Baltimore on River Road is the Atherton Site which consists of a large village and a small mound. The village is one hundred and twenty yards in length and forty yards wide, with the longer dimension corresponding to the edge of a narrow terrace which is aligned on a northwest-southeast axis below a large hill and above the broad Great Miami Valley. The Atherton home, which was built in 1849, stands in the bend of River Road on the eastern side of the village. It was built over part of a low mound, a fact confirmed both by Atherton family tradition and by recent observation. At present, the thirty-six foot broad tumulus is barely discernible on the northwest side of the house. The village (33-Ha.-83), judging by the types of the great quantities of flint and stone artifacts found there, is of Early Woodland origin. Projectile points are predominantly corner notched in the shorter types, while the

---

[1]*History of Hamilton County*, p. 160.

Woodland Artifacts from the Atherton Site (33-Ha.-83) Crosley Township

longer specimens are usually stemmed. Nearly all are of locally available chert and are consequently rather crude due to the graininess of the material. A few large unstemmed blades have been found, but can best be described as blanks. Drills are all short with expanded bases. The celts, grooved axes and pestles found are all rather crudely worked from glacial boulders. The finest piece from the site is a polished stone tubular pipe. One side of the tube is flattened much the way many bannerstones are, which raises some doubt as to whether it was made for smoking or as an atlatl weight. Conspicuously absent is pottery. Its absence from collections, however, does not preclude its existence at the Atherton site since most of the collected material was gathered before concern was shown for ceramics. At present, the quantity of soil washed onto the site from the hill above it prohibits productive surface collecting.

On Dry Fork Creek north of Willey Road is another large village site. Mrs. George Meyer, former occupant of the farm on which the site is located, has a large collection of material from the site. Included in her collection are pipes, pottery and the usual variety of flint implements. The actual village is in the low land on the east bank of the stream south of the point where it is joined by a deep irrigation ditch. Unfortunately, the survey was neither able to inspect the collection nor to find any artifacts on the site itself which could identify the culture of its ancient occupants.

In the lowlands along the main watercourse of Crosby Township have been found at least a dozen circular hearths containing burnt and cracked stones, charcoal and burnt earth. The two discovered and excavated by the survey were in the east bank of the Dry Fork near the county line, and were in every way typical of the others reported. To build a fire on a river bank is surely a natural and common practice. But the discovery of numerous hearths of exactly the same type is interesting in that it raises the question, "Who used them?" Three reports of groups of such hearths have come to our attention, and a fourth group was studied during the course of the survey. At least twenty such hearths have been found buried deep in river banks in Ross County, Ohio; MacLean mentions them in connection with both Butler and Hamilton County,[3] and Dr. Glenn A. Black of Indiana has encountered them in many parts of his state. The East Fork in Clermont County has produced the best examples, all of which can be considered as typical of the class. They are circular and from three to five feet in diameter. Within a circle of small stones (usually sedimentary) set on their sides is an area filled with charcoal, and fire-cracked rocks indicative of the fire which burned the ground underneath to a depth of three inches. The outstanding feature is that no artifacts have ever been found in or around them. In Clermont County they occurred in well-patterned groups arranged in a criss-cross pattern along a middle line with each one approximately twenty-five feet from the next. Mr. Laudeman, on whose land they were found, recalls seeing a

---

[2]*Ibid.*, p. 161.

[3]MacLean, J. P., *Archaeology of Butler County*, Robert Clarke and Co., Cincinnati, 1879, p. 198.

whole field full of them, laid bare by a flood. They were all arranged in the "street" pattern, and were devoid of artifacts.

Although further exploration might prove the hearths to be the products of unrelated cultural groups, that conclusion seems unlikely. But until the charcoal specimens from Crosby Township and Clermont County can be dated by the Carbon 14 test, only further study and field work will shed new light on this peculiar problem.

ADDITIONAL MOUNDS AND VILLAGE SITES IN HARRISON TOWNSHIP

Harrison Township is located in the northwestern corner of Hamilton County. The high hills which abound in the rest of the county are absent here; instead, there are only rolling plains and, in the vicinity of Harrison, low rounded hills. The streams all drain into the Whitewater River which is approximately sixty feet wide where it flows through the southwestern area of the square township. In respect to its topography, Harrison Township bears a greater similarity to southeastern Indiana than to any other area of Hamilton County. This tendency seems to be reflected in the prehistoric populations also, but the dearth of existing sites leaves us with little material with which to explore this possibility further.

The archaeological wealth of the township is mainly concentrated on its western border in and immediately around the town of Harrison. The sites in this area are situated in three distinct zones; the low land on which the business district is now built; the fifty foot high terrace above the town; and the rolling hills beyond the terrace. Our entire knowledge of the sites in the bottoms is gained from Samuel Brown's *Western Gazeteer* of 1817, a guidebook for the immigrants to the new American West. Fortunately, he frequently forgot his task and lapsed into irrelevant but enlightening discussions of oboriginal remains. The following is extracted from the excellent section on Harrison:

> The traces of ancient population cover the earth in every direction. On the bottoms are a great number of mounds, very unequal in point of age and size. The small ones are from two to four feet above the surface, and the growth of timber on them small, not being over one hundred years old; while the others are from ten to thirty feet high, and frequently contain trees of the largest diameters..... There is a large mound in Mr. Allen's field, about twenty feet high, sixty feet in diameter at the base, which contains a greater proportion of bones, than any one I ever before examined, as almost every shovel full of dirt would contain several fragments of a human skeleton. When on Whitewater (river), I obtained the assistance of several of the inhabitants, for the purpose of making a thorough examination of the internal structure of these monuments of the ancient populousness of the country. We examined from fifteen to twenty. In some, whose heights were from ten to fifteen feet, we could not find more than four or five skeletons. In one, not the least appearance of a human bone was to be found. Others were so full of bones, as to warrant the belief that they originally contained at least one hundred dead

bodies; children of different ages, and the full grown, appeared to have been piled together promiscuously..... We discovered a piece of glass weighing five ounces, resembling the bottom of a tumbler, but concave; several stone axes, with grooves near their heads to receive a withe, which unquestionably served as helves; arrows formed from flint, almost exactly similar to those in use among the present Indians; several pieces of earthern ware; some appeared to be parts of vessels holding six of eight gallons; others were obviously fragments of jugs, jars, and cups; some were plain, while others were curiously ornamented with figures of birds and beasts, drawn while the clay or material with which they were made was soft and before the process of glazing was performed..... The smaller vessels were made of pounded or pulverized muscle shells, mixed with an earthen or flinty substance, and the larger ones of clay and sand..... one of the skulls was found pierced by an arrow, which was still sticking in it, driven about half way through before its force was spent. It was about six inches long..... In digging to the bottom of them (the mounds) we invariably came to a stratum of ashes, from six inches to two feet thick, which rests on the original earth. These ashes contain coals, fragments of brands, and pieces of calcined bones. From the quantity of ashes and bones, and the appearance of the earth underneath, it is evident that large fires must have been kept burning for several days previous to commencing the mound..... Almost every building lot in Harrison contains a small mound; some as many as three. (Western Gazateer, p. 57-8.)

If Brown's description can be taken as accurate, both mounds and village sites existed on the bottom land. The only one of the many mounds which he mentioned that has appeared in any recent literature is the one in Mr. Allen's field. Brown's excavation should not be considered as a process of removal but rather one of only superficial digging. Of this mound Dr. Glenn A. Black wrote:

The north second terrace of the Whitewater River, just south of Harrison, was the site of a very large mound which was destroyed fifty-seven years ago during the building of a new road. My informant, Harry M. Cook, of Harrison, remembers The mound and describes its extent as about 75 feet in diameter and 18 to 20 feet in height. He said also that burials, pottery, and ornaments were found during its destruction. This is probably the mound referred to in Samuel Brown's Western Gazeteer in his description of the antiquities near Harrison. .... As there was no other mound of this size in the immediate vicinity of Harrison, and as the dimensions given by Mr. Cook tally so closely with this description (Brown's) there is little doubt that they spoke of the same mound.
Arch. Survey of Dearborn and Ohio Counties, Indianapolis, 1934, p. 186.

Of the others, little more can be said other than that this is certainly an unusually dense concentration of tumuli.

The deep "stratum of ashes" found beneath the tumuli clearly indicates a deposit of kitchen midden. At many of the late prehistoric sites the soil is still so dark that it gives the appearance of being composed of ashes; one hundred and fifty years ago it must have seemed even more so. The charcoal, bones and debris are all commonly found in middens; the fired areas could have been hearths. Brown failed to record whether the pottery vessels were from the mounds or from the debris beneath them, but if they were from the village area, the mounds must be of Fort Ancient origin. From the mention of shell tempered pottery we can assume that a Fort Ancient component existed at Harrison but a more detailed analysis of the shapes, sizes and ornamentation based on Brown's description alone would lead to conclusions too speculative to be of any value.

The second zone is a large level terrace north of the town which commands a broad view of the business district below. The four stages by which the sites that were located there were discovered and reported follow a pattern that recurs all too often in midwestern archaeology. First came the pioneers such as Samuel Brown whose report on this site is even more fantastic than the preceding quotation.

> On the neighboring hills, northeast of the town, are a number of the remains of stone houses. They were covered with soil, brush, and full grown trees. We cleared away the earth, roots and rubbish from one of them, and found it to be anciently occupied as a dwelling. It was about twelve feet square; the walls had fallen nearly to the foundation. They appeared to have been built of rough stones, like our stone walls. Not the least trace of any iron tools having been employed to smooth the face of them, could be perceived. At one end of the building, we came to a regular hearth, containing ashes and coals; before which we found the bones of eight persons of different ages, from a small child to the heads of the family. The positions of their skeletons clearly indicated, that their deaths were sudden and simultaneous. They were probably asleep, with their feet towards the fire, when destroyed by an enemy, an earthquake, or pestilence.
> *(Western Gazeteer, p. 58-59)*

Unusual as this description seems, it should not be completely disregarded, since other pioneer authors wrote of similar structures in the Chillicothe area.

By 1934, mounds in the same area were noticed and measured by trained archaeologists.

> Though just across the state line in Ohio, this interesting group of six mounds is worthy of description. They rise on

the east second terrace of the Whitewater River just on the north edge of the town of Harrison.....
The largest of the six is at present 75 feet in diameter and five feet high. It is in a cornfield and has been cultivated for a number of years. The others of the group lie to the west of the large mound on the edge of the terrace and vary in size from 40 feet to 27 feet in diameter; their height is about 3 feet. All five are in an uncultivated pasture, and all have pits in their center.

(Black, Glen A.; p. 186-7)

The next stage, the recognition of nearby village sites, was performed by Mr. Tony Collins of Hooven, Ohio, who recalls that the terrace was known to collectors for years as a fertile hunting ground. His personal collection contains innumerable Woodland artifacts found there. The final stage has just recently taken place, shortly after the entire terrace was graded for a new subdivision. The survey's visit to the site, although too late to examine either the tumuli or the village, pinpointed the locations of the mounds and learned that immediately prior to the recent construction, they were from two to two and one-half feet in height.

The third zone consists of a shelf of rolling land beyond the terrace. We know nothing of the shapes or sizes of the few small mounds which are known to have been there. A few miles south of Harrison, between Kilby Road and the Whitewater River is the Mary A. Cardan Mound and village. (33-Ha.-144,265) This mound "... was formerly conical, about 20 feet in height and about 70 feet in diameter. It was dug by Mr. Cardan in 1900, at which time he found burned clay layers, graphite, copper bracelets, expanded-center gorgets of slate and "shell pendants".[1] Although Black classified this as an Adena mound on the basis of the artifacts recovered by Mr. Cardan, recent evidence fails to support him, for it has been learned that copper earspools, a classic Hopewell trait, have also been found in the mound. We would hesitate to make any cultural identification until further evidence can be obtained through excavation. The Woodland village mentioned above is across the railroad tracks from the mound. Artifacts from this site are in the Hayhurst and Collins collections.

A final group of mounds is located in the southeast corner of section 16, above Lee Creek, just west of the dividing line between Harrison and Crosby Townships. All of them are so low that the survey was unable to precisely relocate the group after the initial discovery. Their diameters range from thirty to about fifty feet, and the heights do not exceed ten inches. Fortunately, the process of erosion which has reduced them so greatly has temporarily been retarded by revegetation.

ADDITIONAL MOUNDS AND VILLAGE SITES IN WHITEWATER TOWNSHIP

Whitewater Township occupies a roughly rectangular area of 25 square miles in the southwestern corner of the county. It is bounded on the

---

[1]*Op. cit.*, Black, Glenn A., p. 186.

north by Harrison and Crosby Townships, on the east and south by the Great Miami River, and on the west by Dearborn County, Indiana. The upland region in the northwestern portion of the township is the easternmost extension of the chain of hills stretching across Dearborn County; between these hills and the Whitewater River is the valley which widens to a plain two miles broad near the point where it meets the Ohio. Scattered among the hills on the Indiana side of the line are numerous salt licks, among which Double Lick is the most prominent in point of size and archaeological value. Many of the archaeological sites on the western border of Whitewater Township must be considered in relation to their proximity to these salt licks, for by settling around them, the Indian had the two-fold convenience of abundant game and easily obtainable salt. Undoubtedly, an exhaustive examination of the area around these licks would produce evidence of every pre-Columbian and historic tribe which ever inhabited the region.

The first mound which will be discussed is in the northern part of the township just south of West Road near the Miami-Whitewater Forest. (33-Ha.-115) The Blue Jay Mound, named for the nearby community, crowns a hilltop in the midst of rolling upland terrain. On first glance, the seven and one-half foot high tumulus appears to be conical, but a closer inspection reveals a three to four foot wide elevation or terrace on the east and west sides of its perimeter. This two foot high "walk" gives it the appearance of a bell — not in the sense that the term is applied to the English barrows, but in the true sense of a "stepped" cone. Although we can speculate that the terrace was formed by years of plowing, there is as yet no conclusive evidence that it was not intentionally constructed by the builders of the mound. Perhaps it was this phenomenon which recently led someone to dig a two foot deep hole into the apex.

The next group of four sites are in the valley to the east along State Route 128. The first of these is the Bunnell site, a Woodland complex of unknown extent situated on a spacious terrace near the Great Miami River. From the height of the terrace one would think it to be safe from the annual floods, but in the last thirty years the ancient habitation level has been buried beneath two feet of flood-borne silt. Older collectors remember the Bunnell site as a productive source of side-notched points and Woodland pottery. On the third terrace of the river a few miles below the Bunnell site is the Weisbrodt site, a small Woodland component very much like the group along the northern border of Colerain and Springfield Townships mentioned earlier. The village covers the back corner of a level cornfield on the Weisbrodt farm and adjoins a creek on the northern side of the field. In addition to the many flakes, cores and firecracked rock found on this site by the survey, three-quarter and fully grooved axes, and both stemmed and side notched points have been found there in the past. The Weisbrodt collection contains a number of fine serrated projectile points. The entire village area is covered with sandy soil washed from the hill which flanks the eastern side of the site.

On the terrace directly across Route 128 from the Weisbrodt site, at the edge of the Roessler family's land is the Caleb Roessler Mound. (33-Ha.-92) Fifty years ago, when it was listed in Mill's Archaeological

Atlas of Ohio it was between twelve and fifteen feet in height but in 1918 the upper eight feet were graded down to enlarge the arable acreage of field. In the earth-moving process many skeletons and copper bracelets were found. The bracelets remained in the Roessler family for years but recently have been lost. A second segment was removed by the farmer on whose property over one fifth of the tumulus stood but nothing was found at that time. That the tumulus straddles the property line is clearly evidenced by the cleanly shaven profile separating the remaining portion from the next field. The profile reveals load marks when it is scraped and, even at a glance, shows that the stony soil of the surrounding field was not employed in the construction of the mound. When both destroyed parts are taken into account, the original diameter of the mound can be approximated at about one hundred and five feet.

Three eighths of a mile further to the west on Route 128 there lies another sizeable buried village similar to the Bunnell site. In the summer of 1958 the level of occupation was one and one-half feet beneath the modern surface of the terrace. However, shells of mussels, flint, lithic fragments and occasional artifacts fill the overburden to the surface. This village is situated on a long narrow terrace east of a small creek and south of the state road.

The newly built Firehouse in Hooven covers the site of a once sizable mound. (33-Ha.-258) According to Mr. Tony Collins, whose thorough research provides our only information on the mound, it was partially removed in the decade before the Civil War when the open fields were beginning to give way to the new community. While the town was building up around it, persistent erosion wore it away so completely that by the early 1950's, when the Firehouse was being planned, the very existence of the mound had been forgotten. However, no sooner had the bulldozers cut into the ground than human bones were encountered at a uniform level three to four inches below the sod line. Three skeletons were found; all three were the skeletons of adults; one being a female who had died in childbirth. Due to the speed with which the burials were removed by the machinery, no information on the tombs, if there were any, or other inhumation data was obtained. The only artifacts found were four five inch long serrated side-notched blades. All four were made from the same dull black, grainy material and were found on the same pile of bulldozed dirt, but since they were not in situ it is impossible to say whether or not they were originally with a burial.

Dr. Metz repeatedly refers to "cemeteries" and "atteliers" in his surveys of the lower Little Miami Valley. Both terms were borrowed from the classical archaeological tradition of the times and have fallen into disuse in twentieth century American archaeology. It has been fairly certainly established that the atteliers or workshops were actually village sites, but the exact nature of his cemeteries is still uncertain. Undoubtably some, like Madisonville and Sand Ridge, were actually village sites also, but the peculiar locations of others — high hills and sloping land — are completely unfit for habitation. Perhaps this second type are of the same nature as the three which have recently come to light in Whitewater Township.

The first one of these is the Sand Run Site, located on the steep hillside to the north of Sand Run Road a few yards west of Lawrenceburg Road. (33-Ha.-89) The burials were placed in shallow holes which had been dug into the bank of the hill. To date, five burials have been recovered; two of them by a farmer from Cleves who found them while hunting baby ground hogs and three by Mr. Tony Collins who carefully excavated his find. The preservation of all the bones is excellent; one of the three uncovered by Mr. Collins appeared to have been covered with an animal skin fastened at the shoulder with a bone pin. A second "cemetery" was in Section 19 on the top of a long glacial moraine at the base of the hills north of Elizabethtown. Literally hundreds of burials have been found in shallow graves in the sand covered by a four inch thick layer of topsoil. With the burials there were artifacts ranging from shell tempered elbow pipes and shell beads to side notched projectile points and cache blades. The last undisturbed section of this site was recently destroyed by the local gravel companies' operations. The third "cemetery" is discussed later in this chapter.

A large stratified village site stretches for one-half mile along the brow of the terrace east of Lawrenceburg Road. Only on its northern and southern extremities do the evidences of prehistoric occupation come to the surface; in the center, where the terrace projects farthest into the bottoms, the village levels are silted over to a depth of from fourteen inches to three feet. The northern quarter of the site is predominantly late Woodland. Limestone tempered cordmarked sherds, cores, flakes, and the Newtown series of varied point types were found over an area of five acres by the survey. In the middle portion of the site Fort Ancient burials have been found at depths of from eighteen inches to four and one half feet from the surface. Further to the south, where the terrace subsides into the lower bottom land on Lawrenceburg Road is a Hopewell concentration. Flint Ridge points, cores, and flake knives, as well as the usual Miami Fort ware are scattered over the entire terrace at this point.

On the flat plain around Elizabethtown, we find the Elizabethtown Mounds #1 and #2. These lovely tumuli are on the Rennert property on Stephens Road northwest of the village. The larger of the two is perfectly conical and about nine feet high; thirty yards west of it is the second, barely discernible and possibly unrelated to the first. Mr. John Rennert, uncle of the present owner, carefully planted trees on Mound #1, making it a family park and heirloom, but neglected to provide the same preservative for Mound #2, possibly because of its small size. Consequently, although the Elizabethtown Mound #1 will remain intact indefinitely, the other will be completely destroyed in a few years (33-Ha.-25, 26). The sandy field around the mounds produces many white and tan cores of chert but, due to the sparsity of such material, the site cannot be classified as a village.

Another mound is situated on the high hill above Stephens Road, near the center of Section 19 of Whitewater Township (33-Ha.-251). This five and one-half foot tumulus lies directly on the fence line between the Rennert and Guard properties, and is quite well preserved. From its top, there is a completely unobstructed view across the Great Miami to Miami Fort.

One of the more problematical sites in Whitewater Township is on the Butler farm west of Elizabethtown on Route 40. The problem arises from the fact that two low tumuli occur in the center of a distinctly non-ceramic habitation site. The village is near the steep edge of a terrace which runs in a nearly east-west line from Elizabethtown to a point far into Indiana without major projections or irregularities. This is the same second terrace upon which the nearby Elizabethtown Mounds and the Lawrenceburg Road village stand. The perimeter of the area in which occupational material has been found forms a large oblong, two hundred yards from east to west and seventy yards on the line sighted from the Elizabethtown Mounds. Since the survey visited a nearby site many times in the course of the work, it was convenient to give the Butler site (33-Ha.-249) similar attention. However, very small side and corner notched "bird points", scrapers, a grooved axe, and great quantities of roughly worked chert were the only artifacts recovered. Black mentions small points, grooved axes and numerous slate objects[1] but neither the surveyors nor the many collectors who have explored this site have been able to find any indigenous pottery on this otherwise prolific site. This fact is all the more surprising in the light of the presence of two one and one-half foot tall mounds near the center of the oval. One stands to the west and the other to the north of the end of a nearly indistinguishable terrace which enters the village from the northeast. The problem of chronology here is similar to the problem of the mounds at the Turpin Site in Anderson Township; like the former, the Butler mounds may have been built by a later people who resided in a nearby village site.

When looking for a more recent village in the immediate vicinity, one turns at once to the unusually extensive State Line Site, a major Fort Ancient village situated on the Ohio-Indiana border just west of the Butler Site. The actual village area extends one-eighth mile in every direction from the center of the site near the edge of the rolling terrace; within the confines of the village are at least five tumuli while adjacent to the village on the north is the last of the three "cemeteries" discussed above. The physical location of the village has the usual features preferred by Fort Ancient city planners — i.e. a high, level or rolling terrace near a major stream — but unlike some Fort Ancient sites such as Sand Ridge or those below Miami Fort, its location is totally ill-suited for defensive purposes. The greatest value of the location is its proximity to the Great Miami River which now flows nearly a mile to the southeast of the site but formerly may have flowed at the base of the terrace. If this was actually the case, the villagers had a handy source for the great numbers of mussel shells which litter the present surface of the site.

Before discussing the village in greater detail, it will help to examine the typological listing of the artifacts which have been found there:

---

[1] *Op. cit.*, Black, p. 192.

Material found by the present survey:
- broken bone
- broken rock
- 3 hammerstones
- 1 loaf shaped pestle
- 2 double bitted polished celts
- 1 unpolished chisel
- 1 slate tool (hoe?)
- 9 polished celts
- 9 pecked but unpolished celts
- 19 triangular points
- 10 rough, leaf shaped points
- 1 stemmed points
- 1 double based point
- 3 broken points
- 11 large rough points
- 8 scrapers
- 17 cores and blanks
- 1 drilled shell (hoe?)

Pottery, Shell tempered
- 558 plain
- 281 cordmarked
- 13 strap handles or rims to which they had once been attached

Pottery, Grit tempered
- 9 cordmarked

Pottery, Limestone tempered
- 6 smooth
- 12 cordmarked

Material found previously [1]

*	pipes —	limestone, bird effigy; pottery elbow pipes; limestone pipes; slate elbow pipes.
*	other —	small toy pottery vessel with lug handles
*		shell and clay beds
*		two-holed shell hoes
*		abraders
*		discoidal stones
*		drilled celt
*		bone awls
***		one four and one-half inch long triangular point

"..a good specimen of earthern lamp about two inches in diameter, with a handle and degression on the side for the wick." [2]

1... All artifacts marked with one asterisk are in the Collins collection.
All artifacts marked with three asterisks are from the Winter Collection.

2... Gorby, S.S., *The Prehistoric Race in Indiana*, fifteenth report of the Dept. of Geology and Natural History, Ind., Indianapolis, 1886. p. 302.

Obviously, many of these artifacts are out of context if this is an unstratified Fort Ancient village. Among these are the chisels, all of which are of the rather small Lawyer Site variety. The loaf shaped pestle is similar to ones from the Eight and One-Half Mile Site in Anderson Township. The artifact listed as a "double based point" is now broken, but was originally one and three fifths inches in length, one inch wide and thin in profile. The distinctive mark of the type is the two wing-like projections which branch out from the center of the base at an angle of forty degrees. In the entire survey, only two other occurences of this type were noted. One of these was from Sand Ridge and the other from the Twin Mound Village, but since they were both found on the periphery of the respective occupied areas, they cannot be definitely ascribed to the sites or to a specific culture.

The shell tempered pottery is reminiscent of thousands of specimens from the Madisonville focus. The only major difference is the absence of the rare net impressed sherds which were found in small numbers at the Madisonville Site. As to decoration, the unelaborated curvilinear guilloche motif is predominant but both rectilinear guilloches and punctuate elaborations occur in very small numbers. Although the remaining sherds may prove to be of the Newtown fabric, they have not as yet been examined by qualified scholars.

At least five mounds exist within the village area, not including the two possibly related tumuli on the Butler Site a few yards to the east. With one exception, they are all so low that they have escaped the eye of both the casual observer and even of the individual who farms the land. The notable exception is the Hayes Mound, a prominent tumulus upon which the old Abiah Hayes home stands. It is one hundred thirty feet in diameter and stands just north of the state road on the southernmost boundary of the site. It has been dug into at two different times. When the Hayes home was built in 1854, over a dozen burials were removed by the workmen. The present occupant states that the well preserved skulls were set on fence posts and used for targets by rock-throwing boys. More recently, the cellar was modified, at which time a boat stone, now in the Collins Collection, was found. Little need be said of the four other mounds. At least four skeletons were removed from one of them by S. S. Gorby of the then Moore's Hill College, Indiana Department of Geology. The five mounds are scattered at random over the rich alluvial plain, and Gorby did not take the trouble to specify the one in which he had been digging.

In addition to the Gorby excavation, amateurs have frequently attacked the village. The only significant finds known from these excavations are the refuse pits which were reported to the survey by two different local collectors.

One hundred yards north of the habitation area, on the William Stewart farm, was a small "cemetery" which was partially excavated by Messrs. Black and Collins. According to Mr. Collins, who was assisting Dr. Black in his survey work, the interments were found in the exposed sand bank. All of the skeletons were in fully extended positions, and many were accompanied by shell tempered pottery and red ochre. The site has recently been destroyed by the gravel industry.

BIBLIOGRAPHY OF WORKS ON
HAMILTON COUNTY PRE-HISTORY

American Philosophical Society. Proceedings. 1806. Philadelphia, 1884. Transactions, Vol. IV, V.

Atwater, Caleb, *Description of the Antiquities Discovered in the State of Ohio.* The American Antiquarian Society. Worcester, Mass., 1820.

Beckwith, Hiram W., *A Treatise on the Western Indians.* Fergus Printing Co., Chicago, 1883. (Pg. 83)

Black, Glenn A., *Archaeological Survey of Dearborn and Ohio Counties.* Bulletin of the Indiana Historical Society. Vol. XI, No. 7. Indianapolis, April, 1934.

Brown, Samuel R., *Western Gazatteer.* Printed by H. C. Southwick. Auburn, New York, 1817.

Cary, Samuel Fenton, *History of College Hill and Vicinity.* Privately printed. Cincinnati, 1886.

Clarke, Robert, *The Pre-Historic Remains Which Were Found on the Site the City of Cincinnati, Ohio, with a Vindication of the "Cincinnati Tablet."* Cincinnati, 1876.

Cox, Joseph, Sr.; Low, Charles F.; Metz, Dr. C. L.; Langdon, F. W.; *Archaeological Explorations near Madisonville, Ohio.* Journal of the Literary and Scientific Society of Madisonville, Ohio. Part I, 1878-9; Part II, Sept. 1 - Dec. 8, 1879; Part III, Jan. to June 30, 1880.

Day, T. C., *The Antiquities of the Little Miami Valley.* Cincinnati Chronicle. Nov., 1839.

Dickore, M. P., *The Mound Builders of Cincinnati.* Ohio State Archaeological Historical Quarterly. XVIII, (13-27).

Drake, Dr. Daniel, *Picture of Cincinnati.* Cincinnati, 1815.

Force, M. Ferguson, *Some Early Notices of the Indians of Ohio.* Robert Clarke & Co. Cincinnati, 1879.

Ford, Henry A. and Mrs. Kate B., *History of Cincinnati, Ohio.* L. A. Williams and Co. Cincinnati, 1881.

Foster, J. W., LL.D., *Prehistoric Races of the United States.* S. C. Griggst and Co. Chicago, 1887, Pg. 400.

Fowke, Gerard, *Archaeological History of Ohio, the Mound Builders and Later Indians.* Ohio State Archaeological and Historical Society. Columbus, Ohio, 1902.

Giaugue, Florien, *Notes on Various Archaeological Sites.* Harvest Home Magazine. August, 1876.

Gorby, S. S., *The Prehistoric Race in Indiana*. Indiana Reports in Geology and Natural History. Indianapolis, 1886. (Pg. 286-316).

Greve, Charles Theodore, *Centennial History of Cincinnati and Representative Citizens*. Vol. I, Biographical Publishing Company. Chicago 1904.

Griffin, James Bennett, *The Archaeology of the Eastern United States*. University of Chicago Press. Chicago, 1952.

Griffin, James Bennett, *The Fort Ancient Aspect*. University of Michigan Press. Ann Arbor, 1943.

Hall, Joseph J., *The Great American Rosetta Stone, or the Cincinnati Tablet Speaks a Universal Language*. 1949. (No publisher listed.)

Harrison, William Henry, *A Discourse on the Aborigines of Ohio*. Historical and Philosophical Society Library, I, Part 2.

History of Cincinnati and Hamilton County, Ohio. No author listed. S. B. Nelson and Co., Publishers. Cincinnati, 1894.

Hooten, Earnest A., *Indian Village Site and Cemetery near Madisonville, Ohio, with notes on the artifacts by Charles C. Willoughby*. Papers of the Peabody Museum of American Archaeology and Ethnology. Harvard University, Vol. VIII, No. 1. Cambridge, Mass., 1920.

Howe, Henry, *Historical Collections of Ohio*. Bradley & Co., Cincinnati, 1847. Second edition, H. Howe and Son. Columbus, 1889.

James, Joseph F., *A Prehistoric Cemetery (The Madisonville Site)*. The Popular Science Monthly. Vol. XXII, No. IV. Feb., 1883. Pg. 445-458.

Johnston, John, Esq., *Account of the Indians Inhabiting Ohio*. America Antiquarian Society. Worcester, Mass., 1819. (Vol. I, Pg. 271)

Langdon, Dr. Frank W., *Concerning Skeletal Materials from Madisonville*. Journal of the Cincinnati Society of Natural History. Vol. IV, No. 3, Pg. 237-57.

Leonard, Lewis Alexander (Editor), *Greater Cincinnati and Its People*. Vol. I, Lewis Historical Publishing Company, Inc. Cincinnati, 1927.

Low, Charles F., *Archaeological Explorations near Madisonville, Ohio*. Journal, Cincinnati Society of Natural History III. No. 1 pg. 40-68; No. 2, Pg. 128-139; No. 3, Pg. 203-220.

MacLean, J. P., *Archaeology of Butler County, Ohio*. Robert Clarke & Co. Cincinnati, 1879.

Martin, Quimby, and Collier, *Indians before Columbus*. University of Chicago Press. Chicago, Illinois. (Pg. 259-288).

Maurer, C. J., The *British Version of Lochry's Defeat*. Bulletin, Historical and Philosophical Society of Ohio. Vol. IV, No. 3. (Pg. 215-221).

Metz, Charles L., M.D., *The Prehistoric Monuments of Anderson Township, Hamilton County, Ohio*. Journal of the Cincinnati Society of Natural History. October, 1881. Cincinnati, 1881.

Metz, Charles L., M.D., *The Prehistoric Monuments of the Little Miami Valley*. Journal of the Cincinnati Society of Natural History. October, 1878. Cincinnati, 1878.

Mills, William C., *Archaeological Atlas of Ohio*. Ohio State Archaeological and Historical Society. Columbus, 1914.

Moorehead, Warren K., *Primitive Man in Ohio*. G. P. Putnam's Sons, New York, 1892. Pg. 49-58.

Moorehead, Warren K., *The Stone Age in North America*. Riverside Press, Cambridge, 1910. (Contains illustrations of Artifacts from Hamilton County.)

Oehler, Charles M., *Turpin Indians*. Cincinnati Museum of Natural History, Popular Publications Series No. 1. Cincinnati, 1950.

Olden, J., *Reminiscences of Lockland and Reading*. Cincinnati, 1879.

Peabody Museum of Harvard University
1) Report of the Curator. Eighteenth Annual Report, Peabody Museum. Pg. 499-500. 1886.
2) Many valuable manuscripts pertaining to the eastern Hamilton County area.

Putnam, Frederick W., *Explorations in the Ohio Valley*; American Architecture and Building News, Vol. XX, No. 572, Dec. 11, 1886

Putnam, Frederick W., and Metz, Charles L., M.D., *The Marriott Mound No. 1*, Papers of the Peabody Museum of American Archaeology and Ethnology, Harvard University. Cambridge, Mass., 1886.

Randall, E. O., *The Masterpieces of the Ohio Mound Builders; The Hilltop Fortifications*. Ohio State Archaeological and Historical Society. Columbus, Ohio, 1908. Pg. 51-61.

Sargent, Col. Winthrop, Letter to Dr. Benjamin Smith Barton concerning Hopewell Artifacts found in mound at Cincinnati, 1784; in Historical and Philosophical Society of Ohio, Cincinnati.

Short, John T., *North Americans of Antiquity*. Appendix A. Harper Co., New York, 1880.

Squire, Ephraim George, and Davis, E. H., *Ancient Monuments of the Mississippi Valley*, Smithsonian Institute, (Contributions to Knowledge) Vol. 1, 1848.

Starr, S. Frederick, *The Excavation of an Indian Mound in Sayler Park*, Journal of the Historical and Philosophical Society of Ohio, Vol. XVI, No. 1, January, 1958.

Thomas, Cyrus, *The Problem of the Ohio Mounds*, Government Printing Office. Washington, 1889. Pg. 39-40.

Webb, William S. and Baby, Raymond S., *The Adena People, No. 2*, for Ohio Historical Society, Ohio State University Press.

Webb, William S., and Snow, Charles E., *The Adena People*. The University of Kentucky Reports in Anthropology and Archaeology, Vol. VI. Lexington, Kentucky, 1945. Pg. 29-33.

Whittlesey, Col. Charles, and Read, M. C., *Antiquities of Ohio*. Ohio Centennial Report, 1876.

Williams, John S., *The American Pioneer*, Vol. II., R. B. Brooks, Printer, Cincinnati, 1843.

Willoughby, Charles C., *The Cincinnati Tablet — An Interpretation*. Ohio State Archaeological and Historical Quarterly, XLV. 1936. Pg. 257-264.

Willoughby, Charles C., *The Turner Group of Earthworks, Hamilton County, Ohio*, with notes on the skeletal remains by Ernest A. Hooten. Papers of the Peabody Museum of American Archaeology and Ethnology, Harvard University, Vol. VIII, No. 3. Cambridge, Mass., 1922.

Wissler, Clark, *The American Indian*. Third edition. New York: Oxford University Press, 1922. Pg. 16-17.

ADDITIONAL WORKS CITED

Abbott, John S. C., *History of Ohio*. Tyler & Co., Detroit, 1875.

Ellis, Holmes, *The Possible Cultured Association of Flint Disk Caches*. Ohio State Archaeological and Historical Quarterly, Vol. XLIV, No. 2.

Kappler, Chas. J.; (editor), *Indian Affairs, Laws, and Treatys*. Washington, 1904.

Ritchie, Wm. A., *Traces of Early Man in the Northeast*. New York State Museum and Science Service, Bulletin No. 358. June, 1957. Pg. 7.

Webb, Dr. Wm. S.; Elliott, John B., *The Robbins Mounds*. University of Kentucky, Lexington, Ky. 1942. Reports in Anthropology and Archaeology. (Vol. V, No. 5).

Witthoft, John, *A Paleo Indian Site in Eastern Pennsylvania, An Early Hunting Culture*. Proceedings of the American Philosophical Society. 1952. Volume 96, No. 4. Pg. 485.

MAJOR COLLECTIONS OF HAMILTON COUNTY ARCHAEOLOGICAL MATERIAL

Only those collections of considerable size or importance to later researchers are listed below. Practically every village site has at least one collector who considers it to be his personal hunting ground. The only such collections listed are those which contain material not represented in the major collections. Likewise, many institutional collections were not listed because similar material can be found in other, more exhaustive collections.

Private Collections:

Atherton Collection	– Harrison, Ohio
Behrman, Arthur	– Cincinnati, Ohio
Collins, Tony	– Hooven, Ohio
Conover, J. Donald	– Bluefield, West Virginia
Denneman, Robert	– Newtown, Ohio
Fitzpatrick, Gerald	– Bridgetown, Ohio
Fluke, Richard A.	– Terrace Park, Ohio
Garvey, Father Wm.	– St. Xavier, Cincinnati, Ohio
Hayhurst, George	– Sayler Park, Cincinnati, Ohio
Hunt, Norman	– Mt. Healthy, Ohio
Keller, C. Robert	– Cincinnati, Ohio
Long, Carlos P.	– Cincinnati, Ohio
Meyers, Mrs. George	– Mena, Arkansas
Perry Collection	– Miamiville, Ohio
Rittenhouse, H. W.	– North Bend, Ohio
Schlosser, Gene	– Cincinnati, Ohio
Schneider, Edward	– Cheviot, Ohio
Schweizer, Jacob	– Harrison, Ohio
Schwind, Charles	– Cincinnati, Ohio
Ward, Robert	– Madisonville, Ohio
Winter, C. H.	– North Bend, Ohio

Institutional Collections:

American Museum of Natural History	–	New York, New York
British Museum	–	London, England
Cincinnati Art Museum	–	Cincinnati, Ohio
Cincinnati Museum of Natural History	–	Cincinnati, Ohio
Indiana Historical Society	–	Angel Mounds, Evansville, Indiana, and Indianapolis, Indiana
Ohio State Museum	–	Columbus, Ohio
Peabody Museum of Harvard University	–	Cambridge, Massachusetts
United States National Museum, The Smithsonian Institute	–	Washington, D. C.

www.ingramcontent.com/pod-product-compliance
Lightning Source LLC
Chambersburg PA
CBHW030120100526
44591CB00009B/464